THE TIME IS NOW

CONVERGENT
NEW YORK

THE
TIME
IS
NOW

A
Call to
Uncommon
Courage

JOAN CHITTISTER

Copyright © 2019 by Joan D. Chittister

All rights reserved.
Published in the United States by Convergent Books, an imprint of the
Crown Publishing Group, a division of Penguin Random House LLC,
New York.
convergentbooks.com

CONVERGENT BOOKS is a registered trademark and its C colophon is
a trademark of Penguin Random House LLC.

Library of Congress Cataloging-in-Publication Data is available
upon request.

ISBN 978-1-9848-2341-0
Ebook ISBN 978-1-9848-2342-7

Printed in the United States of America

Jacket design by Sarah Horgan
Jacket photographs: (background) Naoki Kim/Shutterstock;
(colors) ngagwang/Shutterstock

10 9 8 7 6 5 4 3 2 1

First Edition

In all my years of traveling around the world, one thing has been present in every region, everywhere. One thing has stood out and convinced me of the certain triumph of the great human gamble on equality and justice.

Everywhere there are people who, despite finding themselves mired in periods of national darkness or personal marginalization refuse to give up the thought of a better future or give in to the allurements of a deteriorating present. They never lose hope that the values they learned in the best of times or the courage it takes to reclaim their world from the worst of times are worth the commitment of their lives. These people, the best of ourselves, are legion and they are everywhere.

It is the unwavering faith, the open hearts, and the piercing courage of people from every level of every society that carries us through every major social breakdown to the emergence again of the humanization of humanity. In every region, everywhere, they are the unsung but mighty voices of community, high-mindedness, and deep resolve. They are the prophets of each era who prod the rest of the world into seeing newly what it means to be fully alive, personally, nationally, and spiritually.

*It is to these average
but courageous people*

who forever seek the truth,
defend the weak,
bring the peace,
and always, always, always, stand up
to protest injustice—
it is to you—
that I dedicate this book.

WHY READ THIS BOOK

With the world around us cracking at the seams and America in a state of polarization and political disarray, this book sets out to answer the most serious questions of them all:

How do we really get out of the swamp we're in?

Answer:
By confronting it.

Response:
How?

Answer:
Truthfully.

Response:
But what will that take?

Answer:
A model, a vision, a commitment, courage, and . . .

Annnnnnd . . . ?

What else is needed to fix this muddled world?

Answer:
You.

CONTENTS

A CHOICE

We have a choice.

You and I stand in a space between two worlds. The first world is the one we were told—and never doubted—would last. The statue of Lady Liberty stood in the bay of the Port of New York and welcomed foreigners to our shores. The Constitution rested on its three-part government, each one serving as a check and balance on the other two, all of them devoted to answering the needs of the entire country. That was then.

Now the statue still stands there but the welcome is an illusion that is too often measured by color and ethnicity. The Constitution still exists, yes, but its interpretation now rests more on the prejudices of partisanship than on universal national concerns.

The second world in which we are steeped, the one we are living in now, defies everything we were taught to expect. Immigrants in dire straits are locked out of the United States. Members of Congress barely speak to their counterparts across the aisle, let alone feel required to respond to their needs. Long-standing international alliances are fracturing. The proliferation of nuclear weapons has raised its ugly head again after years of negotiation—even in countries long considered too small and remote to be a threat to anyone. As Americans, we are the first country to unilaterally violate an international treaty. In our withdrawal from the treaty with Iran that constrained its nuclear ambitions, we undermine international negotiations. A secure and stable national future for a global community can no longer be taken for granted.

We have a choice.

More than that, national borders everywhere are breaking down as entire populations are driven from their homes to find a place in other countries. Yet at the same time, alt-right and far-left political positions are dividing peoples everywhere, threatening local and global peace.

Somewhere between pre-war isolation and a postwar world that put its hope in the power of global institutions, life turned upside down. We became citizens of the world, cling as we might to small-town USA. The planet is now our neighborhood, a polyglot place where very different kinds of people need and want the same things.

We now find ourselves surrounded by people formed in other ways and places who by virtue of their tribes, cultures, and religions see life in other ways than we do. They were raised to value other ideals than we were. They speak another language. They paint a different face on their icons of God. They, too, seek life in its fullness. At base, we are all nothing more than humans together. We all want an order in our societies that we can depend on. We want a good future for generations to come. We want a way to make a steady, decent living that provides the basics of life and a chance to enjoy them. We want the opportunity to become the best of ourselves. Most of all, perhaps, we want a government that exists for the good of its citizens, that protects rather than oppresses its people, that is an equal partner in the community of nations.

Until now, destiny meant the right to get more of the past. Not now. Instead, the diverse cultural and generational makeup in our country does not yearn for the America of the past because they never knew it.

We may all seem to be going in the same direction, but when we get to the crossroads of a world in flux the human parade splits: Some emphasize the need to preserve the values and structures that brought us to this point. Others warn that standing still while the world goes on will be our downfall. So we wander in a world of expectations we can neither see nor embrace.

Breaking news: the world is a land mine of differences.

No doubt about it. The direction we take at this new crossroad in time will not simply affect the future of the United States. It will determine the history of the world. The future depends on whether we make serious decisions about our own roles in shaping a future that fulfills God's will for the world, or simply choose to suffer the decisions made by others intent on imposing their own vision of tomorrow.

This moment is a daunting one. At every crossroad, every one of us has three possible options: The first choice is to quit a road that is going somewhere we do not want to go. We can move on in another direction. We can distance ourselves from the difficulties of it all. We can leave the mission unfinished.

The second alternative is to surrender to the forces of

resistance that obstruct our every step toward wholeness. We can succumb to the fatigue of the journey that comes from years of being ignored, ridiculed, or dismissed for our ideas. We can go quietly into oblivion, taking on the values of the day or going silent in the face of them. This choice, in other words, is to crawl into a comfortable cave with nice people and become a church, a culture, a society within a society. We can just hunker down together and wait for the storm to calm down, go by, and become again the nice warm womb of our beginnings.

The third choice is to refuse to accept a moral deterioration of the present and insist on celebrating the coming of an unknown, but surely holier, future. The third choice is to go steadfastly on, even if we are not sure what we will find at the end of it. The third choice is to follow the path of the prophets of old. It is to echo those who came before us who spoke the voice and vision of God for the world. It is to risk, as the prophets did, not really being heard at all—at least not until long after the fact.

The third choice is a choice that demands great courage. But courage, however apparently fruitless, is not without its own reward. Anaïs Nin wrote once: "Life shrinks or expands in proportion to one's courage." And courage is a prophet's road.

The prophets had a choice.

So do we.

A WORD ABOUT PROPHETS

This book is about the prophet in you. A world gone badly askew stands on the cusp between authoritarianism and freedom, between universal compassion and national self-centeredness. It is a world scarred with violence, institutionalized fraud, rapacious human degradation, political suppression, economic slavery, and rampant narcissism. It is a world in wait. It waits for some wise and wild voices to lead us back to spiritual sanity. Our world waits for you and me, for spiritual people everywhere—to refuse to be pawns in the destruction of a global world for the sake of national self-centeredness.

The only question is, Will we take up what we know is our moral and spiritual responsibility: to make the world a better place for all, to bring to life the fullness of Creation for all? To help bring about equality, safety, security, and compassion for all?

That is where the prophet comes in.

The prophet is the person who says no to everything that is not of God.

No to the abuse of women.

No to the rejection of the stranger.

No to crimes against immigrants.

No to the rape of the trees.

No to the pollution of the skies.

No to the poisoning of the oceans.

No to the despicable destruction of humankind for the sake of more wealth, more power, more control for a few.

No to death.

As Daniel Berrigan, one of the prophets of our time who decried the Vietnam War and turned that into a life-long path to peace for many, said: "The prophet is one who speaks the truth to a culture of lies."

And while saying no, the prophet also says yes.

Yes to equal rights for all.

Yes to alleviating suffering.

Yes to embracing the different.

Yes to who God made you.

Yes to life.

This book is about prophetic spirituality.

And what exactly is that?

It is the spirituality of awareness, of choice, of risk, of transformation. It is about the embrace of life, the pursuit of wholeness, the acceptance of others, the call to co-creation.

It is a way of living with our eyes wide open and our hearts full of fervor for all of life. It is a spiritual legacy that embodies the commitment of Jesus the Prophet and the courage of all those seers and gadflies, the insightful and sensitized men and women who came before him to call for the Will of God for everyone. It is a call to live not only in praise of God but in union with God's will for the world. In short, prophetic spirituality is about living out our faith on the streets of the world, rather than just talking about it.

Faith is invalid unless you are living it. That is the basic message of the prophets and it is as true today as it was thousands of years ago.

Prophetic spirituality is an active spirituality that demands as much rock-hard commitment as it does heartfelt concern.

It's not an easy spiritual path. It can be tiring, wearying, soul-saddening and at the same time electrifying. It sends us into the world with one eye on the will of God for all of it at all times. The biblical prophets of Israel—every one of them—when they came to a crossroad between truth and untruth, when they had an opportunity to settle down, to quit the resistance to evil, to accept what was, chose instead to keep on going. Despite difficulties, they chose to live and proclaim Truth for themselves and for others. The prophets were the sirens in the night, the sowers of far-flung seeds, the eternal agitators in the soul of the people, of the nation, torches in the murk of confusion.

They chose to go on sowing the message of God's will for the world upon which the future rested and the people depended. If they were ever to find their way out of the darkness to which a failed leadership had condemned them, the prophets knew that some truth-tellers, however few, had to keep the message alive.

These prophetic people, people just like us, simple and sincere, eager and inspired—these sheep herders like Amos and small-business people like Hosea, these simple country farmers or priests like Jeremiah, these thinkers and writers and dreamers like Isaiah and Ezekiel, these struggling lovers and suffering witnesses like Micah, these brave and independent judges and leaders, like Deborah and Miriam, made no small choices. They chose courage. They chose the expansion of the soul. They chose to stake their lives on what must be rather than stake their comfort, their security, the direction of their lives, on what was.

It is that steadfast, unyielding, courageous commitment to the eternal Will of God for Creation—whatever the cost to themselves—that is the prophetic tradition. It sustains the eternal Word of God while the world spins around it, making God's Word—Love—the center, the axle, the standard of everything the faithful do in the midst of the storm of change that engulfs us as we go.

What can we learn from all of this? We must decide what to do now in a world reeling in a centrifuge of transformation, metamorphosis, and vicissitude. Like the Israelites in captivity, we find ourselves exiled from a quieter past, thrust into a cosmic village, and plunging headlong into a totally new world both here and abroad.

This book offers the prophetic tradition as a guide as we move from the old ways of life to the eternal burning light of God, whom scripture reminds us "is doing something new" again.

What does the prophetic tradition, the prophetic dimension of the spiritual life, have to do with us? How will it affect our lives? What will it mean to our own development and spiritual authenticity? Most of all, what are the gifts that come to those who hold the Word of God up to the injustice of our own time? Who can we ourselves become if we persist in the pursuit of truth-telling in the face of rejection?

First and primarily, the prophets support tradition but are wary of traditionalism. They know what it is like to be suffocated under the weight of meaningless laws when the soul is crying out loud for a new vision of leadership. The prophets remind us that faith in the living God has often been smothered, even abandoned, by the institutional trappings of the past.

The prophets care about secularism and they preach against the creeping abandonment of God's will for the simple sake of being able to integrate more easily into different communities. They know what happens to a society—and to a church—that forfeits the breadth and impact of its spiritual perspective in its adherence to a single issue religion. They know what happens to the faith when it concentrates only on selected sins and allows sins like social injustice to suffocate, suppress, and silence the rest of the commandments.

Today's prophets understand why whole bodies of spiritual people of every tradition now cluster in intentional communities to find the spiritual sustenance they cannot find in the parish, congregational, or diocesan leaders who ignore all the questions to concentrate on only a few.

Prophets today understand the cries of the destitute and the unemployed, the elderly, the depressed gay teenager broken down by ages of church-defined defamation, the victims of clerical sexual abuse, the rejection of women as full human beings, as full disciples of Jesus, and the ordinary people who look for shepherds in their religious leaders and not ecclesiastical emperors.

The prophets of our era lament the lack of religion's concern for underpaid women, trafficked girls, beaten wives, and the miserable second-classism of women everywhere—in both church and state.

Today's prophets try to deter the ruthless, relentless, systemic violence practiced in the name of patriotism, calling itself "the Will of God."

The prophets understand why spiritual seekers cry out in despair for church leadership in the condemnation of nuclear weapons but get condemnations of condoms and contraception instead.

The prophets care about leadership. They know that civil leaders lay burdens on the backs of the vulnerable in order to make the already comfortable sinfully affluent.

The prophets care about everything average people like you and I care about. Indeed, with all their hearts and at the price of all their security, the prophets care about clerical- ism and condemn it. They care about static secularism and set out to reinvigorate the soul of the temple itself. They care about poverty and decry it, about violence and condemn it, about religion and set out to purify it of its arrogance, its false faith, and the emptiness of its rules and rituals.

And what happens to these prophets, who care more about these things than about the preservation of past power structures? They risk being shunned socially, often ridiculed and ignored. But they also know that the will of God is what brings good and joy and happiness and equality into a world that suffers from the lack of it. And what do they do about it? They go on repeating the Will of God until it is finally accomplished—regardless of what powers set out to stop them. As a result, their lives and stories have become the heart of both the Old and New Testaments, both Hebrew and Christian, both then and now.

They are more committed to the Word of God than they are to acceptance by those who claim to be the guardians of the Word of God but betray its meaning.

They are more committed to commitment than they are to social approval.

They are more given to faith in God than they are to fidelity to the system.

They are more full of hope in the future than they are afraid of pain in the present.

They are more committed to the Word of God than they are to those who speak for the institution but claim to speak for God.

They are more committed to new questions than they are to old answers.

They are people of their times who prefer to stand, if necessary, alone with God.

They live very much in the present for the sake of a future they know may never be their own. And they call us to do the same. They call us to make for our mantra again: "If not for us, then because of us." They call us to cry out, as the great prophets before us did, so that tomorrow the Word of God for all our good may finally, finally be heard.

The prophetic tradition is clear: We are not here simply to succeed today. The prophet will persist for as long as it takes to make the present what God intends it to be as well as to prepare the future to maintain it. We are here to seed the present with godliness so that others may someday reap the best of what we sowed.

What follows in the pages ahead are the seeds of the prophetic tradition. The hope is that they will implant inside you a new life, a new appreciation of others, a new way of living for God that will enflame your heart to change the world. For all our sakes.

The country, the world, needs you.

God needs you, too.

1

RISK

I remember a time when, rather than using the Benedictine model of *lectio divina*—the devotion of sacred reading—the prioress used a book of meditation prompts to lead the community through a period of daily contemplation.

This process of guided meditation was a clear one. First, the leader read an episode from the Gospel. Second, she intoned: "Imagine the scene." Third, she read, "Jesus is walking around the Sea of Galilee, stopping here to cure a blind man, stooping there to raise a young girl from the dead, engaging with some of the local scribes and Pharisees on the fine points of the Law, ignoring the Sabbath to save a donkey in a ditch. The crowds are pressing in on him—pushing and prodding, hands out, eyes pleading for attention, for help. Then he looks up and sees you watching from the margins. 'And you,' he says, 'what will you do for these—simply stand there looking on?'"

This read-and-engage format was an entirely different style of spiritual formation than the one I would deal with after Vatican II and its concentration on liturgy and scripture study. This first approach depended more on immersing ourselves in scriptural narratives—in becoming a character in that particular scripture story—

than in personal deliberation on the presence of God in our daily lives. It revolved more around the development of a scriptural practice than it did on the integration of the Jesus life with my own. Nevertheless, in that brief period of guided meditation, I learned something that would serve me all the rest of my life: Contemplation, I came to understand through this focused attention on individual Gospel passages, was about the immersion of my life in the life of Jesus. The authenticity of my spiritual life, in other words, depended on my grasp of the life of Jesus. That it was to be a personal challenge to my life, as well, would only come later.

That kind of routine reflection did little to encourage much beyond the notion that a life of contemplation and commitment was itself a type of formulaic witness to the Will of God. After all, wasn't it enough to pray regularly? To immerse ourselves in the Gospels? To live inside Jesus' world of first-century Israel and shape our ideals—not necessarily our behaviors or our present choices or our ultimate obedience—around those scenes? Of course it was, we thought. So, our world was neatly divided between church and state. Separated, one from the other, this one in chapel doing daily guided meditations was far superior to secular life on the streets, we thought. That kind of spirituality surely outranked a lay spirituality devoid of something as esoteric as "meditation." Limited in large part to church involvement and rosaries, to religious practices and personal charity, good as those spiritual exercises were, the lay vocation lacked the spiritual aura of the professional "religious vocation." We had managed, in other words, to divide the spiritual life between Christian practice—our prayer routines and "good works"—and Christian witness. Between Jesus the healer and Jesus the prophet. Between acceptable social presence and social transformation.

The separation was both unfortunate and unfounded. The fully Christian life is a blend of both. To opt for sacramental spirituality devoid of prophetic spirituality is to ignore half the Jesus message, half the Christian mandate, half the Christian life.

That the spiritual life was a universally common call, not a graded exercise based on the level of our vocations, was a notion yet to be discovered. What it would mean to the world if both lay and religious decided to "live as Jesus lived" rather than simply go to church was beyond comprehension. It was going to church, after all, that was the measure of our spirituality. It was church attendance and church law, rather than the Gospel and the scriptures, that defined our spiritual responses to life. The very notion of personally responding to public or civic sin simply because you were a Christian had all the confusion of a foreign language. In fact, our very distance from public affairs was itself a measure of the serious Christian life.

And yet, the personal challenge of guided meditation lingered in me for years—otherwise unacknowledged and unresolved long after the final Gospel scene was read aloud in that chapel. It was years before it occurred to me to take the question seriously, What exactly does it mean to live—actually live—a spiritual life? To follow Jesus in a world on the brink of disaster—nuclearism, world hunger, egregious greed, civil breakdown, racial slavery, sexism, and planetary ruin, I began to understand—is surely about something greater than the development of regular spiritual routines or even the lay mandate to be "good Christians."

And so, that question emerges as the nexus of this book. And you? What will you do here and now, in this world, in our time? Simply stand there looking on?

Why? Because underneath it all, something else lingers and will not go away, is still heard in the recesses of the soul and calls us over and over and over. There is another spirituality, far older than guided meditations or spiritual routines, that rings through the ages with models of spiritual giants who knew in their time—and leave to our time—the spiritual obligation to reshape a world run amok.

The question, What will you do? is at the core of spiritual maturity, of spiritual commitment. To follow Jesus means that we, too, must each do something to redeem our battered, beaten world from the greed that smothers it. We must put ourselves between the defenseless and the nuclearism that would destroy it in the name of peace. We must confront the sexism that demeans half the human race. We must redeem it from the anthropology of false human superiority that consumes its resources and diminishes its peoples at the cost of everything on the planet except humankind. And then, as a result, most of humankind, as well.

The poor in our cities sleep rough in the summertime and die of cold in the winter. Our children go to bed hungry. Our women can't walk down our streets alone, for fear of rape, robbery, and mayhem. The rest of the world, caught in the violence of the time, knocks at our gates begging for "room in the inn." And you and I, what are we doing about it? Simply standing there looking on?

The temptation, of course, is to refuse the invitation to really "follow" Jesus—that is, to be in our time as he was in his, to really feed the hungry or contest with the practices of oppression or deny the piety of sexism, racism, and economic slavery. In fact, we often ignore, resist, reject the idea that, like Jesus, we have a role to play in righting a world whose axle is tilting in the wrong direction. We refuse to accept the notion that to turn the compass points of our worlds back to the True North of the soul is what it means to be truly spiritual. Our task is to be "obedient," to keep the laws, the fasts, the dogmas, and the feast days, we argue. But the question we fail so often to ask is, Obedient to what and obedient to whom? Our task is to be obedient all our lives to the Will of God for the world. And therein lies the difference between being good for nothing and good for something. Between religion for show and religion for real. Between personal spirituality that dedicates itself to achieving private sanctification and prophetic spirituality, the other half of the Christian dispensation.

Yes, the Christian ideal is personal goodness, of course, but personal goodness requires that we be more than pious, more than faithful to the system, more than mere card-carrying members of the Christian community. Christianity requires, as well, that we each be so much a prophetic presence that our corner of the world becomes a better place because we have been there.

There is no room here for dedicating a lifetime to maintaining the perfect spiritual routine, the antiseptic moral cleanliness, an acerbic and long-suffering silence alone. None of that, in fact, marked the life of Jesus himself, who "consorted with sinners," healed foreigners, called women to discipleship, contended with scribes and Pharisees about the nature of the faith itself, and irritated the leaders of both the temple and the throne, both religion and government.

Instead, the call of Jesus is the call to prophesy, to speak a word of God to a world that prefers religious rituals and spiritual comfort to the demands of moral maturity. It is to be a prophet's witness in a prophetless place.

Prophetic spirituality calls us to walk in the wake of the biblical prophets of ancient Israel, to hear the word of God for the world and repeat it, shout it, model it until the world comes awake. It is to demand it until the hungry are fed and the sick are cared for and the violent are sent away empty of their power to destroy.

Prophets then and prophets now are those who look at life as it is—hard of heart for many, unfair for most—and set out to expand it. Prophets simply refuse to accept a vision of tomorrow that is limited to the boundaries of yesterday and empty of God's word for today.

The classical prophets of ancient Israel did not rebuild the past. They didn't even really restore the present. But they did hold up a restless, unyielding vision of tomorrow. They made it clear that none of us has the right to quit until God's will for the world is accomplished. Anything less is to ignore the judgment of God.

The voice of the prophets was seldom appreciated by the kings and high priests of their own time. The prophets were ignored by the very ones to whom the messages were addressed, the ones who could have averted the disasters that followed. But they went on proclaiming the Word of God regardless. And in doing that, they preserved the memory of the Will of God for humankind. They went on, however seemingly futile, describing what it would take to bring life to the fulfillment of creation.

No, the biblical prophets were not acceptable to the powers of the time. They were always the voice of the future, the voice of the fullness to come. They were also voices of warning about what would happen to us, to the world, if the world stayed on the road it was on—unless those who heard the word would give their lives to birthing it.

But we must never forget, as well, that the prophets were people like you and me. They were discouraged by the chaos of the present. They were weary from trying. And they also toyed with the same three options that challenge us yet. They had to decide whether they would forgo the struggle entirely, surrender to the prevailing culture, or refuse to agree with the injustice of the time.

No, we are not all prophets—in the classic or original sense of the word—but we are all meant to be carriers of that same prophetic message to our own time. We are meant to be witnesses to a spirituality that is not only faithful to the liturgical dimensions of our traditions but committed, as well, to the kind of prophetic spirituality that cries out again the loud, clear message of God to a skewed and unjust world.

The fact is that there is no one too busy, too old, too

cloistered, too remote from the struggles of the world to have no way whatsoever to promote the Word of God in a world such as ours.

For all of us who live under threat of social degeneracy from the power brokers, the profiteers, the dictators, the nativists, the narcissists, and the prejudiced, there are decisions to make. Shall we do something to reshape the heart and the soul of the worlds we inhabit? Or shall we do nothing and claim that we were powerless in the world? Will we act like we do not know that there are rallies to attend, students to teach, peacemaking courses to take, public legislation to study and discuss, facilities and services to open to the homeless, and, at the very least, honest bidding prayers to say in public in our churches? Will we raise no voice at all in the pursuit of God's will for us all?

What this world needs most from us right now is commitment to a spirituality that is prophetic as well as private, that echoes the concerns of the prophets who have gone before us. Prophecy, in other words, is an essential dimension of Christian presence, a clear witness of the Spirit-directed life.

The problem is that we have lost all consciousness of the biblical prophets and so of our own spiritual birthright. In fact, we might not even recognize them if we saw them. Yet it was precisely for times such as ours that God sent these prophets of old to wake up the world around them to its distance from Truth. It is surely time for this generation to rediscover them.

Indeed, the question rings across the ages: And you? What will you do?

Reflection

There is risk to every life. Those who risk nothing risk much more, the Talmud teaches. While we keep our heads down, our mouths closed, our public reputations unblotted, thanks to the silence we keep in the face of great public issues of the day, the pillars of society erode in front of us. The Constitution flounders against the political ambitions of the very people pledged to protect it. The poor get even poorer. The middle class watches their retirement go to dust. It is to us in this place that the scripture calls most clearly: "Surely God is my salvation; I will trust and not be afraid." We must not fear the darkness; we must simply resolve to carry light into wherever we are.

The call to discern the difference between what is holy and what is simply popular, between what is and what should be, is of the essence of the good life. The work of God is in our hands. To ignore that is to ignore the very fullness of life. Every prophet contemplated the price of the risk and went on regardless—calling to the world to become its best self—and so must we.

"Only those who will risk going too far can possibly find out how far one can go."

T. S. ELIOT

2.

PARADOX

There are two ways to be holy, but you wouldn't know it from the things we say about those who are.

There are people who labor all day in the worst of conditions, for instance, for the neediest people in the world. Call them saints; call them courageous; call them the "salt of the earth." Indeed they are.

Then there are other people who see the conditions in which the neediest people in the world are left to live and they work to see that those conditions are changed. And people denounce them for it. Call them unrealistic. Call them enablers. Call them unfaithful to their country—and even to their church.

Dom Hélder Câmara, for instance, called "the archbishop of the poor," remarked as the government became more and more hostile to his support of the oppressed in Brazil: "If I give alms to the poor, they call me a saint. If I ask why they are poor, they call me a communist."

Archbishop Óscar Romero in El Salvador was also a threat to an oppressive government. Why? Because he was a support and sign of possibility to the poor. So the government assassinated him in his own cathedral while he said Mass. "You may kill me," he said, "but I will rise in the hearts of the poor."

The church later canonized Romero. People call him a saint now. But at the acme of his prophetic posture in El Salvador, the church itself not only did little to protect or save him but also questioned his support of troublemakers as they defied a repressive government.

Prophets can be so irritating. Dostoyevsky is clear about the way the world absorbs them. He wrote, "People reject their prophets and slay them but they love their martyrs." Once the troublemaker is silenced, the public can afford to revere their now tamed selves.

The recurring question about which is the greatest holiness, those who are doers—the martyrs—or those who are the changers—the prophets—is a seductive one. Which is better, people ask, to be prophetic or to be pastoral? Is it more important to do charity or to demand justice? Or better yet, they insist, should religious people really be involved in politics? As if curing the man born blind on a Sabbath was a political act or a pastoral act or a prophetic one.

It's when we try to answer such empty questions that we find ourselves in a maze. Which are better, apples or oranges? Who is holier, those who nurse the Catholic sick or those who build interfaith hospitals for everyone? At the end of discussions like that, all we have managed to do is to reduce the whole Christian enterprise to a series of false opposites. To pit one work against another only dims the real value of each.

However spurious the contest may be, it is nevertheless a continuing question. We like our religions served calm. We call quiet "unity." We avoid discussions about issues that have two sides to them, both defensible, both with a valorous history. Like soldiering and conscientious objection as Christian concepts. Like the role of women in the home and the place of women in the public arena as fully human behaviors. Like ministering to heterosexuals or to the LGBTQ community, for instance. Dorothy Day's answer is itself prophetic: she did both. She refused to choose one over the other. She writes: "What we would like to do is change the world—make it a little simpler for people to feed, clothe, and shelter themselves as God intended them to do. And by fighting for better conditions, by crying out unceasingly for the rights of the workers, the poor, or the destitute—the right of the poor, in other words—we can, to a certain extent, change the world; we can work for the oasis, the little cell of joy and peace in a harried world. We can throw our pebble in the pond and be confident that its ever widening circle will reach around the world."

Dorothy Day brooks no misunderstanding. She is out to change the world. She is also out to feed and clothe and shelter people—"the worthy and the unworthy poor." And she will fight to get it done while she creates little oases of peace everywhere. Then, she says, one little space at a time, she will encircle the globe with this new way of being alive.

That's charity to the ultimate. It is also a world-changing prophetic statement about the Christian lifestyle.

Set in such stark terms, it is easy to see that both dimensions of ministry are strengthened by involvement in the other. What is the use of feeding the hungry without advocating for better social services? What is the use of demanding higher wages for physical labor while omitting the need for childcare for working mothers?

Or, on the other hand, what is the use of prophetic vision while the living poor go hungry? As the world waits for the legislative insight it will take to restructure social services or raise wage levels, a family can starve. Intellectual concern is no substitute for the food a family cannot afford despite the fact that they work two jobs. The truth is that charity is laudable and seldom considered dangerous. It is the sign of the nice person, the one who unloads the trucks or sets up the temporary housing units.

Prophecy, on the other hand, has ragged edges. It sets out to deconstruct the present situation. It critiques social structures to which many have given their lives or in which they have status. They are invested in its continuance. They have something to lose if the world listens to the cries of the prophet for change.

Where the hallmark of charity is its uncommon generosity, the ring of real prophecy lies in its uncommon courage. Both go far and beyond the normal measure of either. Both of them lead the way for others to follow. Both of them give witness to the world of another way of life, a better way of life for us all.

Nevertheless, charity without prophecy can serve only to make the world safe for exploitation. As long as the poor are being fed, why raise the wages it would take to enable them to feed themselves? It enables employers to go on underpaying and overworking the very people who have made them their wealth.

At the same time, prophecy may disturb a society but it does not necessarily comfort it. In fact, it can remain at a distance from the sufferings of the time. As a result, it runs the risk of intellectualizing the problems of the world, which the rest of us can then go on discussing to death.

The great prophets both comfort the wounded and work at changing the structures that embed the wounding to the point that we all come to take it for granted. When that happens, there's little hope of change.

Reflection

As the poet Charles Péguy warns us, "We must always tell what we see. Above all, and this is more difficult, we must always see what we see." When we fail to recognize the injustices of society—to smell them and bind them, to carry the lame and shelter the homeless, we will never bend our hearts to hear them and shout out their cries for all to hear. And change.

"The curious paradox is that when I accept myself just as I am, then I can change."

CARL ROGERS

3.

AWARENESS

All of life is a sacred adventure in the coming of the Reign of God, a journey to fullness of life rather than its denunciation. Yet many still follow the privatization of the spiritual life that blossomed in the nineteenth century. They still cling to the notion that the purpose of the spiritual life is to enable people to flee the sullying secularism of the world for the sake of personal sanctification. It is a spirituality that "practices" religion but does not identify with the Gospel messages that embody it.

If there is anything about the prophetic dimension of life that is clear, it is surely this: more people decline to accept the appointment than to embrace it. As much as the church across time has recognized the role of the prophets as charismatic carriers of the word of God for humankind, as much as prophetic religious groups have left behind them models and ministries enough to rebuild the world from century to century, an old heresy remains. The struggle to escape the world—to avoid conflict and let things take care of themselves—stays strong in us.

We have lost the holy gift of awareness of the world's needs that the prophets brought to fullness. We have overlooked what the prophets knew best: the time most germane to our own sanctification is now. What we do and say, see and respond to, in our own day is the real seed of our own sanctification. It is the times we live in that are our call to courage.

No doubt about it: The purpose of prophecy is to leaven the world, to bring it closer to the Reign of God one small step at a time. The quality of life we create around us as "followers of Jesus" is meant to seed new life, new hope, new dynamism, the very essence of a new world community.

No exception is made for anyone. None of us, however isolated from the rest of life, is forgiven the responsibility. But how can it possibly be done by busy people with family and professional lives to live? The truth is that it's actually not difficult:

1. To be spiritually mature, we must each be about something greater than ourselves. Every local area is being affected by great global movements. The rising price of gas, for instance, can make it impossible for lower-income citizens to afford a car to get to work interviews, let alone to work itself. The price of housing or the lag between a living wage and the cost of living has people living in their cars with their children: no toilet facilities available, no clothes closets, no kitchens or tables on which a child can do homework.

    To own the implications of prophetic spirituality in the Christian life, we must think beyond our own small world to the effects other issues are having on the local area and make a response to them—with others or alone.

2. Prophetic spirituality requires us to think and study

about causes as well as consequences. We begin to ask why people are sleeping in metro stations in the richest country in the world, why in my small town there are not enough beds at night to shelter people from the snow and cold. I ask why there are no funds available for college education for average students. We begin to refuse to take reports for granted and begin to look for answers instead.

3. Prophetic spirituality leads us to understand our own role as "herald in the camp," the watchman of which Isaiah speaks when he repeats his call to prophesy: "I have made you a watchman for the house of Israel; whenever you hear a word from my mouth, you shall give them warning from me." Today's prophets take it as their responsibility to explore what it means to run a hedge fund; to bundle debt; to argue for the right to discriminate against those who are gay, for instance, on religious grounds. Most of all, they set out to help others understand what's going on so we can all do something about it together.

4. The seeker who understands the place of prophetic spirituality in a mature Christianity takes responsibility to spread the word. She holds seminars or article discussions on the topic. She distributes material that outlines and explains the articles so that others can become comfortable with the topic, too.

5. The prophetic Christian identifies with the issue. She becomes a lay expert on the questions and concerns of people with whom she or the community comes in contact. She cries from the housetops about it as did the prophets of old.

6. Most important, the Christian who recognizes the fullness of prophetic spirituality enlarges his own life, at least in small ways. He recycles materials. She wears hand-me-down clothes. He refuses to use chemicals to grow things. She rations her own uses of water. They hold book discussions in their own home. They change their diets in solidarity with native peoples who are losing their grazing lands to agribusinesses around the world.

7. The local messenger of God's Word of justice for the poor becomes known as the oracle on an issue. He does his best to follow new material, to write short pieces for the local newspaper on current issues, and to lead adult discussion groups on those issues as well.

8. Prophetic spirituality requires us to stop hiding behind a life of prayer as an excuse to do nothing about anything. On the contrary, it is the cry of the prophets crying through us that is the measure of our commitment to the prophetic dimension of the spiritual life.

9. It is these little bands of contemporary prophetic spirituality that invite people from every group of "new Americans" in town to talk about their lives and their hopes with local people. They link the two groups and enable them to work together. They know that if boundaries are not allowed to grow up between ethnic groups, they can't develop later into barriers.

It has been said that every community needs at least one prophet. The poet Mary Oliver may have written the best definition of what it means to be a prophet in contemporary spirituality. She writes, "Instructions for living a life: Pay attention. Be astonished. Tell about it."

Reflection

Maybe we should start by writing Mary Oliver's instructions on every church wall. Then we might be alert enough to notice when the first refugees are sent away, when the first inner-city schools are closed, when the first suburban bus routes are removed, making it impossible for poorer people to get to work outside the inner city. Maybe we could even start telling people about it who do have the power to change things. Then, surprisingly, we could take our own place among the prophets of our time.

> "The whole idea of compassion is based on a keen awareness of the interdependence of all these living beings, which are all part of one another and all involved in one another."
>
> THOMAS MERTON

4.

INSIGHT

Prophetic spirituality is an attitude of soul. It is not a set of spiritual "practices," a collection of dogmas, however time honored. The person with the soul of a prophet sees what the rest of the world either cannot see or does not want to see, and uses that vision as a compass through life. The prophetic spirit comes to see the world as God sees the world—and responds to it accordingly. Like the biblical prophets of old, they speak peace for the nations, justice for the oppressed, equality for humankind, care for the earth, dignity for all, and holy integrity rather than control or corruption in the transmission of the faith.

The eyes of the prophet burn through the dross of appearances and set the will of God aflame in our midst. Maimonides, the twelfth-century Jewish philosopher and astronomer, wrote: "The whole object of prophets is to declare that a limit is set to human reason where it must halt."

The thought stuns: Human reason, Maimonides is arguing, can only take us so far. Then, at that point, "holy irrationality" must, if we are ever to become fully human, take us beyond it. It takes us beyond the economic notions of a profit-driven world in which only those who work have the right to eat. It interrogates the idea that only those who have the money to pay extra for it can have heat in their homes for their children or otherwise the electricity will go off. It challenges the political stringency that only those who are like us have the right to live somewhere besides a refugee camp. It debunks the notion that those who call themselves envoys of God always embody a godly message. At some point human compassion becomes more important than commercial competition and racial or religious criteria. Then, as Jesus wept over Jerusalem, so do the prophets of today weep for those caught in the web between profit and prophecy. Clearly, prophetic spirituality teaches the Word that is above all other words. Those who hear it begin to look differently at life than other people do, and so upend the expectations of the world.

The prophets of every age and all ages, Maimonides is telling us, dream dreams far beyond what the average person of that time declares possible. The prophets of our time, like the biblical prophets before us, know that peace is essential, and join groups whose work is to move us toward that point. The prophet believes that justice is achievable, that despite all our differences, we can become community again. So the prophet refuses to divide people into white and black, Republicans and Democrats, Americans and foreigners. In the face of those who say that those goals are too high, that such hope is unreal, the prophet refuses to be silent. These carriers of prophetic spirituality now go on trying to change the ungodly opinions of an unseeing world. So, to the rank and file of humanity, prophets look mad. They look wild.

They look out of sync with the rest of humankind. They look mesmerized by the view of another world.

And it's true. Prophetic spirituality is grounded by the vision of an unseen world where all things are in harmony and where the Will of God for creation is the energy that drives it. They are the saints of Holy Madness, these ones, who like the biblical prophets, like Jesus, see beyond the boundaries of the reasonable to the edges of the imperative. They see that the marginalized—the immigrants, the refugees, the poorest of the poor, the handicapped, the invisible women—can learn and must be taught if they are ever to take their place in a developed world. They know that the starving must be fed or the humanity of the rest of us will waste away before our very eyes. They know that violence in the name of justice is a sham. They come to proclaim another way of being alive, of becoming fully human, of righting a tilting and dizzying world. And the wise know that that is sanctity, not madness.

Prophets come in every age announcing the Good News again: peace on earth, good will to all.

In fact, the early founders and foundresses of religious life—the political martyrs and lay missionaries, visionaries and serious seekers, as well—saw the vision, heard the message, knew the feeling of being more part of the human race than of any particular tribe or clan or religion or nation. They set out for lands foreign to those satisfied with this one to speak another vision of the world—lands where gender didn't limit a person's development, and money didn't define the level of a person's education.

They went into slums and barrios, into filth and disease, into pockets of illiteracy and ignorance. They went anywhere and everywhere something was needed but few people did anything about it and nobody who should have cared did. They went to be the sign of the One who calls all of us to oneness and by embracing "the least of these" made us all one. The Jesus they know moved with drunkards and sinners. He healed the outcast and the enemy. He gathered women as well as men to his side. He chastised leaders who overlooked the poor; he defied the doctrine of sexism that religions use to make male ministers superior, powerful, primary. He stood up and in a clear voice declared wrong any policies of either sacred or secular—church or state—that burdened the backs of the powerless and crushed the spirits of the poor.

The present-day prophets who follow such a One as this know that being unreasonable is the only reasonable way to the Gospel. The reasonable of our time argue that hiring at minimum wage is necessary to keep multi-billion-dollar businesses afloat. They insist that it is reasonable to expect the poor to support themselves, even when there are no jobs for which they can possibly qualify. They say it is only biologically reasonable that women are made to concentrate on domestic issues, despite their individual intellectual talents. Because, after all, God made them that way. As if God made them nothing else at the same time.

Prophetic spirituality of every era proclaims the call of Jesus, whose irrational Gospel is the only really just and sensible and rational thing around: Jesus raised both the living-dead and the dead-dead to life. He sent women to announce the Word as well as men. He criticized the Temple laws that made money changers and their ill-gotten profits a part of what it took to praise God. He protested for the poor who were being exploited. Worse—or better, as the case may be—he questioned the very laws of the Sabbath to the face of those who were justifying and teaching and applying them. Prophets, we learn quickly, want to make sure that there's no misunderstanding about what disturbs them.

Today's prophets of a prophetic gospel know that doing what the world calls "good" rather than what God calls good will do you little good at all.

But where are all of them now, these torch carriers of the Light, at a period in which we need them so badly? In a time when refugees carrying bundles of clothes and arms full of babies are stumbling down railroad tracks and clinging to overcrowded boats in a roiling Mediterranean Sea, where are those who cry out for them to be saved?

The temptation, of course, is to quiet down such a rowdy set of messengers. The temptation is to be "reasonable." "Rational"—as our governments are rational. As if wanton death and deprivation are reasonable. After all, they argue in response, what good does it do to make a stir in the city square or on the steps of the church, right? It will only annoy the rest of the people even more.

The pressure to be quiet, to let other people—the politicians, the neighbors, the "experts"—say how we feel about things is very effective. We shy away from subjects that invite social derision, like guns and militarism and health insurance for everyone. We avoid discussion about topics like the place of women in the church. We stay nice. We allow the degradation and the danger to go on without a word of doubt, without a touch of despair. We challenge nothing and everything goes unchallenged. We become both the victim and the victimizer.

The silence is deafening as the world waits for those on the edge of the crowd to speak up, to speak out. Until someone demands answers, the questions will go on being muted by false gentility, for the sake of social approval, for a false public peace.

But if everything is so right already, so just, so "good as it gets" now, what possible harm can some good universal conversations about it possibly be? About gun ownership, for example. About fossil fuel levels, for instance. About the need for the electoral college in a technological world, maybe. About the need to cooperate with countries smaller than ours in a global world, surely. Ask young people, like the students at the scene of one more major gun massacre, where being quiet, good, nice gets you when the powerful simply turn their backs.

Better yet, prophetic spirituality asks, Who will require that we raise to the level of public discussion the most revealing questions of them all: For whom are things really good? And why? And how did it get that way? And who is being most advantaged by it? Most of all, what is to be done about those for whom the present state of well-being is slipping closer and closer to the murky bottom of life?

The scriptures are clear about the kind of conversations Jesus raised in the Galilee: "At the Healing Pool at Bethesda, there was a man," the scriptures read, "who had been ill for thirty-eight years. When Jesus saw him lying there, he said to him, 'Do you not want to be well?' (It was known that those who entered the pool when the waters were moving would be cured.) And the sick man answered him, 'Sir, I have no one to carry me down; while I am on my way, someone gets down there before me.' And Jesus said to him, 'Rise, take up your mat, and walk . . . ' And immediately the man became well . . ."

The question is, Who is it now and here that is waiting for us "to carry them down" to find shelter, to get care, to learn a trade, to get them childcare while they work, to house the homeless, to reach out to refugees, to open our arms to the world? Most of all, Who is asking that question of our own public institutions? Aloud, bravely. Without care for their own public self?

Reflection

What do today's prophetic witnesses see? They are the ones who look around and ask—however irritating the question is for the rest of us—why so many are so wanting in so wealthy a place. They are the ones who spend their lives proclaiming—madly and wildly, it seems to those who prefer the silence—that justice will not come until the rest of us demand it.

Who are these prophets? They are the ones for which the world waits now. They are those who, like Maimonides, know the point at which the rational has reached its limit. They are you and I. The only question is, What will you and I do to cry out what we are looking at and bring Holy Madness to life—for all our sakes?

> *"You cannot swim for new horizons until you have courage to lose sight of the shore."*
> —WILLIAM FAULKNER

5

AUDACITY

The eternal icon of the prophet occupies the corner of my desk. The gaunt wisp of a figure, arms thrown wide, head up and shouting to the sky, looks to the casual observer to be made of heavy lead, just right for a person of power and influence. Granite-like, it is the very model of an imposing personality, a presence to be reckoned with. I knew several people who fit the type—Teresa of Ávila, Dan Berrigan, Dorothy Day, Rosa Parks, Martin Luther King Jr. So it never occurred to me to question it. At least I thought I understood what was being said in it—until one day I picked it up. As impossible as it may seem, the statue was almost weightless. It lay in my hand as quietly as a piece of cardboard—and may well have been made of it, for all I knew. Whatever the substance—lead or papier-mâché—there was nothing to it. The figure was empty.

And then I understood. So, too, is the prophetic spirit empty of everything but the Word of God, of everything but what it means to be true to the coming of the Will of God for creation. This is the person who is intent on the giving of the self to something greater than the self. There is, in fact, no self here, no personal or self-serving agenda, no egoism. This is the person whose life is compelled by a vision others either do not see or who have yet to commit themselves to something beyond their own agendas.

Two women, both prophets themselves, explain the situation best, I think: Catherine of Siena said centuries ago, "Proclaim the truth and do not be silent through fear." Dorothy Day said in our own time, "Don't worry about being effective. Just concentrate on being faithful." Prophetic witness is not about the aggrandizement of the self or winning awards or being accepted socially. The prophets of our time are singularly and exclusively about being fearlessly true to the Word within.

First and foremost, a real follower of Jesus the Prophet is faithful, forever endures. And endure a prophet must. No new idea, however right, however much the essence of goodness, overgrows old ideas easily or quickly. It took over two hundred years to abolish slavery; more years to abrogate segregation; and now, it seems, even more years to extinguish the racism that is at our historical roots. The Western white has enslaved blacks, dominated indigenous peoples, subjugated women, driven Muslims out of Catholic Spain, and persecuted Jews. Nevertheless, the prophetic promise of a world of equals never died out. The hopes of the human heart once aflame were impossible to extinguish. Generation after generation of prophetic people rose up century after century to speak a word of justice. The fact is that in our own time, we must do the same. In us grows the seed of God's new hope for a world technologically united but spiritually, socially at odds. The prophet's motto, I think, must be: "If not for us, because of us."

Second, the prophet does more than denounce evil. Instead, prophetic spirituality envisions a world in which justice and equality, peace and community, are the norm rather than the struggle. It is the prophet of our time who leads the way to the development of an alternative vision of life by imagining a new normal. Today's prophets prepare for the reconstruction of society by imagining the achievable and drawing others to see it as well. Vision is the first step toward change. Or as the poet e. e. cummings put it, "The first act of creation is destruction." The old order—decaying and disturbing—must go in order to make room for the new.

There the prophet in the midst of us raises a sign of the possible for others to see and own and emulate. The prophet knows that no single group or person can feed the entire world, for instance. But the modern prophet also knows that no act of public voice, no commitment to public care, is ever without impact. The very audacity of envisioning a world beyond the present gives birth to the notion that the desirable is feasible. Then who can contest its doing?

Third, basic to everything is the fact that prophetic spirituality trusts in the grace of holy audacity, the prophetic movement of the Spirit within us, the obligation to tell the truth. To see the truth requires that we must say what must be said, whoever it is that denies it. It takes no small amount of courage to speak a different truth, to ask a different question than is common to our peers, to our family, to our social class. It means cutting oneself off from everything that has formed us, from everyone who depended on us to maintain the old order of things.

It means becoming someone else in the very face of those who hold the old order most dear.

The shock of it all can be life changing, even isolating at times, uneasy always. Social invitations may well slow down awhile for those who disrupt comfortable conversations—at least until those conversations become mainstream. Job promotions may become more scarce while the world around us decides if such ideas are real. Most of all, the circle of friends too often narrows. To speak nuclear disarmament in a region whose industries depend on it, to argue for the rights of women at the Old Boys' clubhouse, can separate a person for life from those who prefer old ways of thinking.

But prophetic spirituality comes with the grace of boldness. Prophets do not tiptoe around truth nor do they distort it or exaggerate it or embellish it for the sake of being heard. The truth itself is enough. The truth itself commits us all to something better. Bold witnesses do not set out to create the public peace when the peace is bogus. They simply challenge the establishment with the bare truth. Then, if the system defends itself or if the system makes no response at all, prophets gather new groups with new ideas to plant the seeds that will supplant the old. They strike out to create what seems to some to be the very antithesis of peace. They protest the strip clubs in residential areas, perhaps, or advocate for protective legislation for sex workers. They organize boycotts of clothes and shoes and toys made by child workers around the world who are being paid seventy cents a day for products that are then sold in developed countries for hundreds of dollars each. They do not shrink from opening the conversation. They are the spiritual gadflies of societies built on inequity and the voice of peoples trying to be heard. Their sound echoes off all the mountains on the planet.

Most of all, they judge no one. They argue only for change, not for conviction. They attack no persons and assume that all of us operate out of good motives but that some of us are bogged down in destructive ideas.

Finally, they do not despair. They know that God's time is not our time. They understand that change comes in seasons. Saint Paul is a realist. Some of us plant, he says. Then, the next generation waters. All of us hope that the harvest is soon. But in the course of its long, slow coming we do not fail in our faith that the Spirit of God is with us and God's time is near.

So what will bring it? Only the commitment of our prophets to hold themselves and their communities to their vocation to embrace "the prophetic dimension of the church." For that, prophets proclaim a Gospel truth and are not silent through fear.

What Thomas R. Kelly calls "the meek and mild mediocrity of most of us" gives way to the drumbeat of justice coming slowly, perhaps, yet inevitably—for the poor, for the outcast, for the forgotten. For us.

Reflection

It is finding the courage to utter the first word of truth in public that takes all the strength we can muster. It is learning to say, quietly, unequivocally, "I think differently about that," and then explain why. It is stepping up to the issue and claiming the right to think differently about it that turns heads and opens hearts. It is not an attack on anyone; it is simply a declaration that there is something missing in the God-life we claim to live. It is the call to consciousness and conscience.

> *"A ship in harbor is safe, but that's not what ships are built for."*
> —JOHN A. SHEDD

6.

AUTHENTICITY

From ancient times to the present, prophets in every society have been routinely vilified. Called strange. Called extremists. Called traitors. Called agitators. Called bizarre. And most of all, called to "Be careful. Be patient. Be nice." while our most invisible sins fester in our midst. Despite the fact that scripture is painfully clear: "If the bugle gives an indistinct sound," Corinthians prods us, "who will get ready for battle?" What antidote to social sin, to godlessness in government, to throwaway populations of forgotten people will ever be able to be heard if no one shouts their name?

It's a cloudy list of labels at best. To be "mad about life" seems a bit heady but amusing. To be an "extremist" in a time of extremism is at least chic. To "revolt" against the status quo tastes of personal independence. But to be an "agitator" in a time of complacency—history is obvious—is a gift to the whole society.

Prophets, for instance, have an important history in the United States. Our prophets spent years of commitment to abolition, to the suffragette movement, to ending war, to curbing nuclear proliferation. Today the list is even longer. Our prophets cry out for a new consciousness about climate change and preservation of the oceans. In the name of creation, they resist the extinction of animal species. One human being to another, they march in the streets crying out for the care of refugees in a globe on the move. Religious communities, churches, and intentional groups for whom the very definition of commitment implies a prophetic stance in the face of moral deterioration of the society around it are prophetic by nature. They know that prayer and prophecy must be soul mates. Otherwise, either their prayer life will simply be formulaic or their ministries will shrivel for want of a living Spirit within them.

At the same time, prophetic spirituality, the public disclaimer of social evil by spiritual groups in the name of religious ideals, has itself just as often instead sunk into a kind of pious indifference. The signs of it are clear: "That issue is political, not religious" we begin to hear as groups attempt to divorce spiritual obligations from political policies. Or, we hear "That's not our role" as groups attempt to justify the distance of spiritually defined groups from social issues. As if what happens in the world around us is no concern of spiritual leaders. Or we hide behind a false humility: "Other people know better about those things," we say with the kind of "humility" meant to excuse us from responsibility for the human race.

No biblical prophets ever said such things, even when they doubted their own ability to articulate the issues as well as others might. Instead, the prophets were clear to the point of outrage about the place of spiritual testimony in the public arena.

"Amos, for instance, prophesied when Israel was at the

peak of its power and stuffed with prosperity. The people had failed, he argued, to admit to themselves on what they were basing their prosperity. He cited for them the wealth that had come to Israel from "war crimes and tax foreclosures" and "failures at the gate" where the elders sat to hear cases but themselves gave evil judgments.

"Do not seek out Bethel," he told them. That is, don't bother to visit the shrine.

"Do not go to Gilgal," he cries. Making pilgrimages will not forgive turning a blind eye to injustice.

"Do not journey to Beersheba," the site of sacrifice, he insists. No sacrifice can save you now, he implies. "Instead," he says, "let justice reign at the city gate."

It is a searing attack on false piety, on those who oppress the poor on one hand but give to religious institutions on the other. To those who ignore the poor on one hand but wear prayer beads on the other. Or worse yet, on those who pretend to be "religious" but do nothing for those for whom the advocacy and voice of religious people are their only hope.

Amos, too, calls us to examine the roots of our security. He prods us to ask ourselves what we do to advocate for justice for the least of them. He calls us to acknowledge the underpaid we see around us, to share our own property and resources, our personnel and money, for their advancement. He insists that we begin to see.

It is impossible to ask what prophetism demands of us now unless we look today square in the face and ask what is missing that we must attend to because no one else is doing it.

Understanding the present—its ills and its sins—is of

the essence of a prophetic spiritual life. To be a follower of Jesus and ignore those who sit blind by the side of the road calling for help because, we say, we are too busy to do anything, unmasks our commitment to comfort. The question is not, What *are* we doing? the question is, What *should* we be doing in this time and on this day and in this particular situation?

The question is not, How can we do it all? The question is, Do we do any small thing to participate in binding up the wounds of the world?

The prophet Isaiah decried the barbarism of professional militarism. Armies used ramps now to breach a city's walls, battering rams to break down city gates, honed bows to kill the unwary, trained and disciplined armies to launch against enemies and slaughter their innocent. Through it all, Isaiah despaired. Israel, he cried, "ate, drank, and made merry." They ignored the human needs around them. They celebrated the defeat of others. They gave up the pursuit of human community for the sake of inhuman power.

Irresponsible affluence and egregious corporate greed, xenophobia, and malicious militarism anesthetize the modern mind as well. What would it take for religious prophets of our own time to risk their own public approval to call upon the soul of the nation in a global world to see its obligations differently? Globally. And, if it is a spiritual mandate, why aren't religious groups doing it?

The biblical prophets challenge us day after day: For whom do we rise up in our own communities? And what do we do about it? And who knows it?

What do we do in the face of global corporations that

use international labor but pay pauper's wagers? What do we say when national legislation puts tax burdens on the backs of the poor? What articles do we write? What prayer vigils do we keep? What legislators do we lobby for change?

We live in a nuclear world. What religious groups teach, as Pope John XXIII did, that "nuclear weapons are a sin against creation," not simply an innocent military option? We live in a rapidly overheating world. Who of us who call ourselves religious, in pursuit of a spiritual life, speak, teach, petition, or boycott companies whose greed is the root cause of these life-threatening policies? We live in a world whose understanding of gender and sexuality is shifting. Who of us support the need to bring more women to the decision-making tables of the country, more transgender citizens into the public arena politically and socially?

More important, what do we think the spiritual life is all about, if not such care? When religious groups opened schools in countries where education of the deprived was not the standard of the time, that was prophetic even if not overtly religious. When spiritually oriented groups began the hospitals, it was a prophetic act to care for indigents no government supported. When spiritual men and women went into the barrios to organize the poor, it was a prophetic act to be a voice for the voiceless.

It is a moral moment again. Every moment is a moral moment, because every moment involves a decision. The point is that we cannot now stop asking these questions and be authentically spiritual. To neglect to pursue the social sores of our own time, to omit taking these kinds of public steps in a world of growing populations and ev-ermore creeping destitution, and yet to go on declaring ourselves to be spiritual people who are "protectors of the poor" has got to be spiritual game playing. Jesus goes on asking every generation unremittingly, "And you, what will you do?" We cannot see injustice and say nothing, do nothing. Not if we are really to be authentically spiri-tual rather than simply pious actors in the game called "church."

John Ruskin wrote, "To see clearly is poetry, prophecy, and religion all in one." It is of the essence of poetry to expose the unseen. If our spirituality is real, if our hearts are true, seeing demands a prophetic response. If our souls are the souls of a prophet, wherever we are we stand up and speak a word of God in behalf of justice, peace, and the poor. Whatever the price we pay for doing it.

Reflection

Prophecy is nothing more than Christianity at its best. It is John the Baptist "making straight the way of the Lord." It is Jesus contending with the Pharisees about the keep-ing of the Sabbath. It is you and I trying to make a stand against a society where money is flowing to the top while the poor languish for the necessities of life at the bottom of the ladder.

We are called to live the Word ourselves, to say a prophet's word, so that others may live better lives be-cause of us. Otherwise, we use a standard that does not really describe the truly spiritual person in the Judeo-Christian tradition. It is little more than camouflage for religious comfort, for making a spa out of the religious life, for confusing a feel-good following of Jesus with the hard work of tending to the world. After all, God did not finish creation. God created us to do that. To abandon and discard the very people, ideals, creation, and commitment we are meant to care about, what kind of spirituality is that? Right. Almost none.

"Lying is done with words and also with silence."
ADRIENNE RICH

7

SUPPORT AND WHOLENESS

Those who would speak the truth of the storm from inside the center of it cannot expect to live without being tossed around by winds. The one who speaks a message other than the official one, in any institution, cannot expect to be loved by it. Institutions live to preserve themselves. Prophets speak to reform the institution. It is a collision course of the heart.

The truth is that institutions are important foundations of any society. But it is also correct to say that the prophets of every society are the watchdogs of its institutions. When the institutions lose their way and ignore their own reasons for existence, they become the problem rather than the solution to social ills. When governments balance their military budgets on the backs of women and children, unwittingly, perhaps, but truly nevertheless, they themselves become the oppressors of an unwary population. Then it is the prophet's responsibility to sound the alarm.

Institutions are forever alert to their traitors for fear that exposure of an open wound would upend the entire enterprise. Churches, for instance, punish prophets who cry foul of them. They hide pedophilia because the institution and the sacredness of clericalism is more important to them than the children who suffer. They choose rigid compliance with church laws on the exclusion of divorced couples from the sacraments and so deny them spiritual comfort along the way. Women they dispose of as secondary to God's plan for discipleship despite even the model of Jesus and his openness to women as spiritual leaders. Governments stiffen when outsiders tell insider secrets. The un-Americanism of American war ethics, the revelation of the CIA's history of interference with other governments, the attack of one department of government on another: all corrode American solidarity. Congress does nothing except politicize fights for partisanship, not justice for all. Corporations sue people when the words of whistle-blowers cut too close to the truth.

On the other hand, onlookers, witnesses, are often reluctant to tell a bitter truth for fear of the wrath that will follow the telling of it.

So why do it? Why would anyone risk unmasking the mask that deceives and so denies the world its innocence? Because we must. Because to allow evil to flourish is the greatest evil of them all. Because, as the rabbis say, "To save one life is to save the world."

"Mystical language," Gustavo Gutiérrez, Peruvian Liberation Theologian, wrote, "expresses the gratuitousness of God's love; prophetic language expresses the demands this love makes." And the demands are many. It is one thing to see the spiritual life as the mystical path to God. It is dishonest to deny, even to ourselves, the demands of its prophetic dimension. One without the other is simply impossible; one without the other is embarrassingly incomplete. In the link between these two dimensions of genuine spirituality lies the wholeness of Christian life.

Prophecy can be a very lonely task. There is little or no public applause reserved in the house of the emperor for those who announce that the emperor has no clothes. For those who understand the need for prophetic spirituality, the spiritual path to the future is a narrow one under any circumstances. To realize that both aspects of the spiritual life—both the sacramental dimension and the prophetic dimension of spiritual commitment—must fit within the boundaries of the soul brings spiritual maturity where once religion for its own satisfying sake dwelt silent and alone. But once the trumpet is sounded, it becomes a single-minded journey from that day forward.

What prophetic spirituality most demands is the strength to go against the very crowds that have formed you. The spiritual town crier begins to speak a language different from that of the surrounding society. There are arguments to explain and ideas to defend. Everywhere. Always. The people who think they have always known you—teachers, pastors, school friends, coworkers, even family—are confounded by the shift in direction. Dismayed by it.

Worse, once the public word is said, it cannot be unsaid. It is also not a neutral word in this place, at this time. You are suddenly a "feminist," with every fringy behavior the stereotype implies, when, actually, you are at most a friend of women, who believes that unequal pay for equal kinds of work is unfair. Even unjust, in fact. You have become a "pacifist," the one accused of cowardice despite the fact that it takes a great deal of courage to speak for the innocents who have become the fodder of modern warfare. You have become "Green" and worry now about the effects of Big Oil and being blacklisted from every job you seek. You have become a "unionist" and suspect the tactics of Big Business. What's more, you have started to say so. The positions come out of centuries of mistreatment and mismanagement yet still take hours of time to explain. So the explanations shrink to a few words and the circle of listeners dwindles as well. People become polite rather than personally concerned.

It is a bitter time for those who have risked so much already to begin a conversation commonly long needed, long ingrained. It is a desolate time, often friendless, always fraught with tension. It is a time when community support—the support of a community of prophetic truth-tellers—is the only answer to a heart darkened by the cost of telling the truth.

If the prophet is to be sustained through the long process preceding the rise of public concern for a problem already too long ignored, four elements cry out for attention. Only a strong spiritual life, good friends, distance from the issue, and laughter really bring balm to the heart and renewed strength to the soul.

Only immersion in God suffices for the strain of rejection. God is the one companion who understands the feeling of emptiness that comes with repudiation by those from whom we had the right to expect support. Prayer—the cry of the psalmists, the image of the beleaguered but imperturbable Jesus—serves to remind us for what great cause we do so bold a thing.

God alone then becomes the lifeline that holds us up in the face of such resistance. The Word of God becomes the fuel of our faith, the ground upon which our hope relies. The Will of God for the world gives purpose to such a simple, bold, and naked approach to truth. It is this new relationship with God that gives us direction, that stiffens our knees for the trek.

At the same time, friends, good friends, the kind who can be equally comfortable talking the problem to death or not talking about it at all, can reduce the price of such loneliness to nothing. Because the companionship is open, loving, caring, strong, there is no subterfuge needed here. There is no need to pretend to be strong where weakness is its own kind of grace. There is no arrogance where weakness is allowed. There is no temptation to be brittlely brave. We can just be ourselves with no stress, no debates, no criticism, no expectations.

Friends are those who love us enough to trust what we're doing even if they themselves have yet to fully understand the implications of it. Instead, they talk to us and with us and for us. They ring us round with a sense of security. They make life with all its confusion possible.

Friends such as these keep us grounded in reality. They provide the space and the sense of emotional stability that contemplation demands. They give us the space to rethink it all, to ask ourselves again what life demands of us, what morality demands of us, what courage demands of us. In touch with the innermost motives of the soul once more, it becomes obvious: there is nowhere to go—but on. Surrounded by love and trust, failure is no longer either an option or a possibility. Loneliness is no longer an obstacle to truth telling.

Friends are imperative, yes, for obvious reasons. But separation is just as much a balm as people. Regular distance from the issue—places where the problem can't intrude—reminds the prophet that, beyond this struggle, life is still life. This, the prophet is reminded, is simply one part of it. Beyond this moment lies the rest of what it is to be fully human. And the rest of it is made for singing alleluia, not groaning.

And finally, laughter, the "delete button" of the heart, clears the system of the dross of the day. It brings a new perspective on life. It says, loud and clear, that there is a world out there that is still full of light and love. Carrying that light, love, and laughter into the world around us as we go can only lighten the load. Even better, it shines a beacon on what is waiting for the rest of the world, as well, once we all determine together to renew it.

Reflection

The question, of course, is, How do we know that we have support and that the support is true, that a new future is pending and a new future is coming? The answer is just as clear: the prophetic act always brings the world to breakthrough. Nothing ever stays the same after the prophetic soul rises up and says her truth. Then everything is in upheaval, true. But then, just as surely, eventually, finally, new light descends into the darkness and people begin to see. Then the human enterprise can inch once again toward the Reign of God. The Word has been spoken and, at least by some, heard. Clearly, when the average, insightful, everyday prophet speaks, the Vision of God becomes present again and creation takes another leap forward.

"When you come together with your other half, you immediately experience a sense of wholeness and completeness."

ANDREW COHEN

8.

SELF-GIVING

Mother Maria Skobtsova, an Eastern Orthodox monastic, lives at the core of the prophetic mind-set. She wrote, "I am your message, God. Throw me like a blazing torch into the night, that all may see and understand." There is very little else to say about the real prophet, the truly prophetic action, than this. It is this Word that rings in every soul. It is the call to be a truth-teller.

But, oh, there are a good number of things in today's electronic world that would like to pass for it.

Mother Skobtsova touches all the elements of what it takes to be authentic in a world that play-acts at everything. In this era, we watch con men define themselves as wealthy when their accountants know that they owe more than they could ever pay. We watch politicians posturing from one interview to the next, pretending to have answers though nothing changes for the people they serve. We see television personalities posing as experts, as if they really had the influence with which they're credited. We watch bureaucrats in big cars pretending to be important. We see resident critics come and go, waiting for the "next big thing" to analyze and destroy before we even get a chance to try it. It's all show.

There is something sad about the sight of it. It makes

us ask over and over again, What is it that is really real? Is all of life virtual now, seldom actual, always part scam, part play?

Clearly, this world runs on image and these images are stock now.

Still, the world goes on, yearning for the genuine. We'd like a real voice on the telephone. We hope for real truth in advertising. We want real wood and real stone and real people and real honesty. It's all important. Yet it's all rare these days. Very rare.

So it seems important to look carefully at what a genuine prophet is and what constitutes a prophetic act so that all the images do not confuse us, so that we insist that all our own protests are themselves the real thing.

A prophetic act aligns the world with the Will of God—even if ignored in the public field of play. The prophetic soul walks in the footsteps of Jesus, who contested with the Pharisees about laws that violated the greater traditions of the Torah. Jesus contested the corban, for example—a temple tax that served to free a younger generation from caring for their elderly parents as long as they donated to the Temple. A clever piece of religious chicanery, it defied the commandment to "Honor your parents" and enriched the pockets of the Temple staff, instead. That kind of struggle between the Word of God and the hypocrisy of those who pretend to be just—but are not—has been the basis of popular protest for centuries.

Committed to follow Jesus the Peacemaker, many Christians protested the alt-right rally to unify the white nationalist movement. But always peacefully. Years earlier, in the search for equality and justice,

American blacks and their white supporters walked in mass movement across the United States, being beaten and broken and murdered as they went but not bruising back. In the next decade, many Christians protested the death penalty in the name of Jesus the Merciful but did not set out to destroy the state itself in compensation. Some refused to pay taxes that were being used to fuel a national war machine. Others contested the legalization of abortion as a sin against the commandment "Thou shalt not kill" but refused to harm doctors who performed them.

In all these cases one thing is plain: the prophetic act is designed to return the people to consciousness of the law of God. But the prophetic act itself does no harm to others. On the contrary.

The prophetic act is always done for the good of others: To save lives in unjust wars. To save fetuses from wanton destruction. To save punishment from becoming nothing more than an act of civil revenge rather than an act of rehabilitation. To bring integrity to the state and justice to its citizens.

In this century, where resources—labor, food products, minerals, fuels—are being leeched from poorer parts of the world to even more enriched developed ones, the stakes are higher than ever before. A few corporations in every category control the flow of goods and the percentage of profit everywhere. We live in one massive, modern feudal system again. But this time it is armed to the heavens.

We live, as well, in the midst of a series of prophetic actions, actions designed to get universal attention, to bring pressure for change, to alert the world to the danger within. A release of photos showed the torture tactics of the modern world, including in the United States, which foreswore it but used other countries to do our torture for us. Then, thanks to the prophets of the time, a flow of secret documents exposed the political skullduggery of nations whose governments were otherwise seen as benign. Average people camped out in public squares to bring a spotlight on autocratic governments and banking practices that impoverished the already poor. The Mothers of the Plaza de Mayo broadcast the disappearance of their husbands and sons around the world for years. The calls to the human community about trees and oceans and pollution and rape and human trafficking, both adult and child, have come from a tsunami of modern prophets.

And in all these cases, the prophets of the time bore the punishment that comes from the systems whose dishonesty and human damage they exposed. "Do no harm" became their holy anthem.

The question is, Where are you and I—the bearers of a prophetic spirituality—in the midst of it?

The prophet always seeks the greater good, the Will of God, and the protection of the people. Those are its hallmarks.

At the same time, there is nothing prophetic about becoming what we say we hate. There is nothing godly in murder and mayhem, in doing damage to people and property, in bringing chaos and anarchy while we say we seek peace and justice. The prophet sets out to address an issue—not to annoy, irritate, and disgust the people whose attention is key.

The prophet is loud, clear, and nonviolent. There is nothing self-serving in the actions of the prophet. On the contrary, prophets almost always suffer loss of social status and an increase of personal rejection, not to mention the legal punishment of the governments they confront. They pay the social cost imposed by societies still blind to their own violence, yet unconscious of their own social sins. And they do it to expose the systemic roots of the violence they confront.

The prophet does not set out on such courses of action in the interests of self-aggrandizement. These are not publicity seekers who are looking for personal fame. They do not put themselves in such physical and social jeopardy to achieve a kind of cheap and useless fame. They are not out to make a profit from their risk of personal reputation and welfare.

Most of all, the prophet is not impetuous, not a rabble-rouser, not emotionally overwrought or psychologically unbalanced. Instead, the prophet is deeply immersed in the spiritual depths of the tradition. They are fueled by the prayer that prays "Do unto others what you would have others do to you"; they give up a part of their own personal life to improve the lives of others and bring the world back to the Will of God for it. The prophet is a living example of the spiritual life with a purpose as large as the life around it.

The questions for spiritual people today are simple: What message do people get from us? What sky do we light up so that others may find their way to new peace and clear justice in a violently unjust world?

Reflection

The prophet in us is not an agitator, an anarchist, a traitor. The prophet calls us to the best of what we say we are. The prophet confronts us with the deep-down great goodness of our common call to holiness, to love of neighbor, to commitment to the life of the whole world. The prophet does not seek conflict and violence and disorder. And when these come, they come down on the prophet's own head. But what greater image is there, as Jesus says, as those "who lay down their lives for their friends."

> *"Let us sacrifice our today so that our children can have a better tomorrow."*
>
> A.P.J. ABDUL KALAM

9

PATIENCE

It's easy to wax eloquent about the place of the prophet in the conscience of the community and the development of society. It's a little more difficult to explain how that development happens. In fact, history is quite obvious: it often never happens until long after the prophet who started the movement has disappeared from the scene. And therein lies the problem. Prophetic spirituality is not a badge to go looking for self-satisfaction if what you mean by self-satisfaction is either success or status.

Two things are relatively clear about the process of prophecy. As Jean de La Fontaine wrote, "Patience and time do more than strength or passion."

To begin with, however, prophetic spirituality is rife with criticism and conflict. Prophecy implies a stretching of the status quo. Whatever life was like before the prophet raises a voice, it will never be the same again. Change begins with the first clamor of discontent and disapproval. After that, the subject can never be suppressed again. The silence is over. All the attempts at innocence are over. With that single outcry, one of the great masks of society has been removed; the conspiracy of collusion has been shattered. The veneer of equality, the pretense of justice, or acceptance, or freedom, for instance, has been rent in two like the veil in the Temple on Good Friday.

It sounds across the nation when one woman refuses to give up her "colored person's seat" to a white man. It starts when the first student refuses to be drafted into an unjust war. It begins with children who stand up and refuse the false arguments politicians and gun sellers give them about making available the weapons that are killing them in their schools. It rises up, strong and steady, when the community gathers to protest the death of one more unarmed young black man.

It is the moment at which the world turns on its axle and looks at itself, yes. But first, it hears the voice of the prophet, loud and clear, pointing out a new and holier path. The criticism comes swift and sharp, of course. "Who are you to talk like this?" the system demands to know. "Don't you dare try to take our rights away!" the comfortable demand. "You won't get away with this," the powerful promise. As quickly as the warning comes, everything the truth-teller says gets dismantled, gets rebutted, gets scorned or, at very least, rebuffed. The reaction of the system is palpable, visceral, swift, clear: "Get rid of these outliers. Drive them out, if necessary. Silence them at all costs." Why? Because the prophet has dared to tear away the veil that hides the face of evil everyone already knows is there but refuses to expose. Where there is little or no personal necessity to face an issue, people avoid it.

To engage in a discussion about what we do not intend to alter is itself a tacit admission that there is something worth dealing with here. And we can't have that.

So everyone turns away, pretends not to hear the question or to see a problem or to consider a question worthy of attention. So we refuse to discuss the root and power of terrorism and simply keep sending more and more young men to die in an effort to stamp it out. Or we refuse to deal openly and rationally with the question of the inequity of women's wages or leadership abilities and create second-level working families or rudderless corporations instead. We argue that we're not racist but won't talk about why our prisons are overfull of black men for things white men do and never get arrested for doing. We keep women on the fringe of worship while we won't talk about the distorted theology of women in the church.

The list of blatant contradictions in society is both major and continuing. Yet there is little or no discussion about the irrationality of those parts of life that time and tradition have made unassailable: It is the birthright of every citizen to have guns of every kind, we contend, even though no case can be made for shooting deer with a military level automatic weapon. Refugees who come from the most non-Western parts of the planet cannot be trusted because they are different from us, even though we all came from different places or that once upon a time Catholics in the United States were as feared as Muslims are now. Capital punishment is a deterrent to capital crimes, we insist, despite the fact that states without capital punishment have fewer murders than those that do. Nuclear weapons are an expensive but necessary part of national security, we say, however many resources are lost to other dimensions of life—medical care, educational opportunity, social development centers—because of our stockpiling thousands of them.

People who engage in these issues, who advocate for these changes, who open these discussions, feel the resistance immediately. The cry in every case is a simple one, basic to the faith, we say, but earthshaking nevertheless: Scripture tells us, "Whatever you do to the least of my brethren, you do to me." The way we treat or ignore or fail to support the voiceless and powerless in society is, in fact, the very issue Matthew's Gospel says we will be judged upon. But the response comes back: "Not on our block," the neighbors say. "No soup kitchen across from our school," the parents say. "No houses for the homeless in this section of town," the local councils say, all of them good churchgoing Christians. All of them proud of it. They give donations to the church. They get their children confirmed. They are active in civic charities. But they say nothing about the relationship between character and conscience in the presidency.

Then, there is the other part of the process to consider. The prophet must learn to be self-critical. How was the message presented? How much preparation went into proposing the project to the people? What else could have been done to prepare them? What must be done now so that both the mentally handicapped and the homeowners on that block can be comfortable?

Being right, the prophet must learn, is not enough to justify being insensitive. Nor is it effective. In the end, the tensions remain, the people on both sides of the divide feel rejected and the Word of God becomes a bludgeon rather than a blessing.

Be aware: patience and time have lessons for everyone involved in situations like this. Historical time tells the world that the major issues of life do not go away. They emerge from one generation, one culture to the next, because the melding of differences is of the essence of community building. Community building, this integration of differences, is the universally human enterprise. Better to resolve them together than to live the short time we have on earth perched on the sharp edge of conflict.

Patience says to stay the course. The questions can go on for months. The dialogue surrounding each will be important. It is important to understand that the slow pace of the conversation is itself part of the spiritual growth of a community. It is only when the conversation never starts at all that the very welfare and spiritual integrity of the community is threatened.

Community is a necessary dimension of patience and time. It's when we pray and meet and discuss and support one another in our simple, powerful actions that we are most able to bear the heat of the prophet's day. It's fear of the unknown that lights the tinder of fear. Leafleting can upset people because they do not want to read the other side of the concern. Town meetings, articles in the newspaper, and the publication of proposals are enough, in many instances, to build a mighty wall of resistance. Which is exactly when the prophet must face that wall with the greatest degree of sensitive, yet implacable, resolve.

What will happen if we do?

There are two basic facts that undergird the prophetic

process: The first is that the prophetic message never really disappears. Issues remain until they are resolved, however many years or lifetimes that may take.

The second is that people grow slowly. It takes time for all of us to learn to live together as mature human beings. In Atlanta, the prophets of desegregation refused to leave the white lunch counters until Georgia was desegregated. In Poland, they never stopped marching for solidarity even when they were threatened with clubs and jail time. In Ireland, they went house to house talking to one person at a time as they struggled for the civil rights marriage equality would provide.

Prophecy is a matter of dialogue, of education, of process, of patience. Not force. The message grows on us. And the soul grows, too, it seems, but only an inch at a time.

Johann Wolfgang von Goethe said, "Against criticism a man can neither protest nor defend himself. He must act in spite of it and it will gradually yield to him."

Sadly but only gradually. After the ground has been prepared and the seeds planted, this harvest of good can break through old, hardened soil to bring new life, new bloom, new nourishment for the world. To raise a voice in prophetic announcement that God is doing something new again is not a vocation for the weak and the fearful, the unconscious and the uncommitted. It is not a vocation that dodges criticism by being sure to do nothing, say nothing, and be nothing.

The voices of the great prophets of the Hebrew Testament still ring throughout the world. The image of Jesus, the prophet, walking from Galilee to Jerusalem contesting with the keepers of the Law, healing the sick on the Sabbath, and raising invisible and socially worthless women from the dead prods us yet to the vocation of public conscience and personal commitment. Without it, what can religion possibly be about except, of course, the salvation of the self—and that, in the face of God's intention that we are to be one another's keepers—is a paltry purpose indeed.

Reflection

For those who believe that the spiritual life is a commitment to personal comfort, social security, and public respect, the task of the prophetic is too great, the life of the prophet is too dangerous, the call to prophetic spirituality too much to ask. Still, for those who realize that the spiritual life is about the following of Jesus the Prophet, nothing else is possible. There are those who, like Samuel Johnson, know that "great works are performed not by strength but by perseverance." After all, the voice and life of Jesus has been a contradiction to a politicized Christianity from the first. The only difference is that it is our turn now to carry the message.

> *"Every great dream begins with a dreamer. Always remember, you have within you the strength, the patience, and the passion to reach for the stars to change the world."*
> HARRIET TUBMAN

10.

FAILURE

When Barack Obama held a televised town hall meeting on the subject of gun control—legislative action repeatedly blocked by the National Rifle Association—his frustration did not lie in the fact that the two opposing groups could not arrive at a compromise bill. The sense of defeat lay in the fact that the other side didn't even show up to discuss it. To be made invisible is to be made impotent. To me marginalization is a death far worse than death. Ask any woman whose concerns have been sidelined, ignored, for centuries. Only now is there the slightest notion that women, too, must be heard.

There is a fate more painful, more humiliating, than the public display of loss. While a vote against a new idea is slim but determinative, there is at least an awareness that a consensus for change is alive and possibly growing. On the other hand, when a group simply laughs a new idea off the stage, when the very thought of a genuine conversation is ignored, when the town meetings are scheduled but no one comes—except the public voice of the issue and a friend or two—the effect of being soundly dismissed is smothering.

What people do not understand they tend to disregard; what they understand but do not like, they tend to disparage. Neither group makes much of an effort to examine either the ideas or the circumstances that underlie new ideas. It is a commonplace of human history.

Too often before an idea is even seriously considered, it is commonly discounted. The proponents of visionary policies are routinely dismissed, in fact. The reason is clear: what the seekers seek is some kind of change. What we're doing isn't working, they warn us. Change is not much acceptable to the powers that be, the powers that profit from life skewed and kept soundly suppressed.

Those whose degree of control or public influence depends on old ideas cringe at the very thought of debating new ways of doing things. Those who make their livings off the money made by such systems resist change with all their might. Ideas are disregarded en masse, not because anyone bothers to prove them unworkable, but because no one considers them at all. You want to raise the minimum wage? Impossible. You want to pay women and men the same amount of money for doing the same job? A ridiculous idea! You want to reduce the hold of the military-industrial complex on the soul of the nation? Maddening! You want "patriotism" to mean something more than willingness to go to war? Shameful. You want your religion to rethink the groundless theology that sustains the male priesthood? Heretical!

And the Old Guard laughs. As Edgar Allan Poe wrote, "To vilify the great man is the readiest way little people can themselves attain greatness."

In biblical times, prophets were often run out of town. In today's society, they are usually simply defined as "eccentric" or "unrealistic." Or, worse, "quaint" throwbacks to another age, this era's odd person out, a socialist, a communist, a feminist—a label. Most, at least here in the West, aren't persecuted; they aren't jailed anymore; they aren't executed or shunned. They are simply ignored.

Marginalization is a dangerous thing because it appears to consider a panoply of new ideas but doesn't really. It simply finds them faulty before finding them debatable, ideas not to be addressed at all. A total waste of time.

So the old world grinds on, no better than before, more deeply deficient than ever. Those whose hearts tilt tenderly toward things become viewed as piteously out of touch, charming perhaps but irritating, sincere but useless.

Both the prophetic voice and the prophetic community of those who band together to become a voice, a force in society, are regularly belittled, demeaned, discounted. So what to do then? When the discussion is real, there is at least a chance that some hearts will warm to the possibility, to the imperative for change. Yet, when the ideas are simply ignored, when no sparks fly at all, when, without a word, the public moves back to the tried and true, the old and empty, the irrational but familiar ideas that have long ago failed, the apparent defeat is complete.

The people lose interest. They withdraw their support. The number of those faithful to the continuation of the conversation dwindles. Abraham Joshua Heschel calls it "uncanny indifference." All the signs were there to support the prophet's warnings, but the people knew better: ignorance was more preferable than public disfavor. So the story of the biblical prophet Isaiah is illuminating.

Isaiah, aware that few listened anymore to his warnings, that his concerns were not much noticed, withdrew to train the next generation of prophets. Isaiah builds for the long haul.

Marginalized and demeaned, he simply continued his work, more sure than ever that Yahweh's word is true and will not be dismissed. Instead of withdrawing from the field, he simply began to work differently.

The message is clear to the rest of us. The prophetic insight never wanes, even when it is not wanted and despite the fact that it is not being heard.

It is a deeply spiritual moment for public truth-tellers. When our work does not succeed externally, it is time for the internal work of the Spirit to become more important than ever. It is time then to double our efforts for spiritual depth. Or we will never be able to go on in the face of disparagement.

This is the moment for the stripping of the self. It is the time to abandon all expectations. This is the point at which to remind ourselves that this reading of the Gospel in the face of the circumstances of the time is God's work, not ours. This is the moment at which we are being called to trust God alone.

By now it is clear that it will not be our strategies, our contacts, or our social connections that will carry this work to fulfillment. It will not be people in high places who save this work. It is in God alone that we must put our trust, abandon all our ambitions, and simply allow things to evolve as they may. While, inside ourselves, spiritually, we become even more prepared to pick up God's work again and go on.

In these periods, like the monastics of the desert centuries before us, we go into the cave of the self and fill it with God alone. Only then shall we have the new energy and the necessary spiritual nourishment we need to face the long days alone in the noonday sun. Only then, rested and refreshed, can we begin the work again.

Reflection

There is no such thing as failure in the journey to the Reign of God. Despite the rejection of today's doers and shakers who want to do less and shake up nothing at all, the prophet wins the day, shaking up one heart, one Gospel at a time. Those who do not do the journey can never know the beauty of discovering what it means to be beyond the greed, outside the violence, beyond the entrapment of smallness of soul. Better to fail, in fact, than to have missed the freedom of heart that comes with speaking Truth to those who seek to smother it. To follow the path of the prophet is to discover what it means to live driven by the wind of the Spirit to complete the work that the greatness of God has begun.

"You may have a fresh start any moment you choose, for this thing that we call 'failure' is not the falling down, but the staying down."

MARY PICKFORD

11.

VOICE

Martin Luther King Jr. said, "Politicians will always ask the question, 'Is it expedient?' but the prophets must ask the question, 'Is it right?'" The words shake convenience, complacency, and comfort to dust. It is convenient to satisfy the crowds. It is complacent to meet the barely satisfactory in human needs and assume that is enough for anyone to do. It is comfortable to know that anything more than nothing will be sufficient to satisfy the record of success. Yet, none of those are enough to give human dignity to the poor. They are hardly likely to provide a decent life to the children of the next generation. No real comfort comes to anyone from the drip, drip, drip of peace and justice. That's the "throw them a bone" politics of the modern world, a little bit for everyone, never more than that to anyone. It is just enough to keep the groundlings quiet.

The words of vision, on the other hand, give life. Visionaries talk about "rightness" for everyone. A right kind of life. The right level of justice. Most of all, the right criteria used to determine what a right life looks like and what constitutes enough justice to truly be justice. Is a right kind of life just enough food stamps to stay barely alive or is it decent housing, education, and medical care,

too? Or, is it "just" to compensate a person for a major in-
jury but not to provide lifelong care for the person? Otherwise the accident victim cannot possibly do more than
sit in a chair for the rest of her life. Is that "right"?

For the prophet, the right criterion to be applied to
the whole of the human journey is the Word of the God
who wishes us, scripture says, "well and not woe." It requires that from one end of the social scale to the other,
we each have available the measure of life's resources we
need so that being alive is a blessing and not a burden.
In my 260-square-block neighborhood, one hundred per-
cent of the children are not fed three meals a day. Who
can call that "right" in a country where two-thirds of the
rest of the population expect clean air, fresh water, dry
beds, warm food, fresh vegetables, good bread, and peace
and community where community claims to be?

When it does not happen, when people mock and
make the fool of those who seek those things, where can
the prophets of our time go to recoup the energy it takes
to survive such a loss? Where do our prophets get the
energy and the will to go on trying, even in the face of
defeat?

The only defensible shelter we have, where hope lives
on despite the strife of the present, is the memory of generations before us. These are the generations of ancients
who struggled for and won the contest for rightness in
Israel. In Israel, the memory of division in the ways re-
turnees from Babylon worshipped without the Temple
as opposed to those who had been allowed to stay in Israel after the war threatened both unity and faith. Yes, in
the beginning they resisted the new ideas of those who

returned to Israel from exile in Babylon with a broader idea of both God and what it meant to be chosen. Little by little they ultimately came to realize that the openness to the rest of the world that their ancestors had found in Babylon was indeed more right than the institutionalization of enmity. As a result, Israel became a force throughout the world. They passed down to us a record of their trials sung by psalmists in Babylon so that we ourselves might have grounds someday to keep faith with the God of the future.

It is the history of the prophetic tradition—right up to and including the prophets of our own time—that is our witness to keeping faith when there is no obvious reason to go on believing. Expedience, the acceptance of what's possible rather than commitment to the continuing struggle for what's right, may allay the ills of the world temporarily. It will not, however, move society another inch toward the Reign of God. Only deep-down faith in the spiritual magnet in the human heart can do that. Only the certainty that God's will for justice and equality trump self-centeredness and greed in human evolution can do that. Those are the most hard-won, the most precious inches of all. They are the inches that may not change society in one swift blow, no. Nonetheless, they are the inches of new ideas that prepare hearts for the spiritual odyssey of a lifetime and so eventually change the world for us all.

Jeremiah confronted the national religion of the Israelites, those who said that the presence of God was guaranteed in Israel. Jeremiah argued, instead, that the presence of God depended on the character of the people, not on the presence of their shrines. It is an insight still being contested to some degree by every people who think that their religious doctrines give them the right to destroy everybody else's. But, thanks to Jeremiah's insistence, that blasphemy can never be made a substitute for goodness again.

Ezekiel saw Yahweh's glory shining above Babylon— the enemy of Israel. God, Ezekiel brought us to understand, was not a private commodity, did not belong to any one people, was life-giver to us all. We are all the children of God, we came to know, no matter who tries to argue otherwise. Most of all, as a result we must protect even those who are different from us.

Psalmists sang the songs of the poor across time. They gave us the awareness of the eternal presence of God. They argued the companionship of God through pain and powerlessness everywhere. They taught us as no other that God is with us always.

Then came Jesus, the One who models for all of us what it means to live outside the norms of a society that has forgotten its soul. He did justice for Samaritans, for Romans, for sinners in the very face of injustice. He spoke the language of equality in everything he did. He laid down his very life in the cause of healing the outcast, commissioning the women, raising the weak to life again, and cleansing the temple. He left a path for us to follow, whatever its ends, however rejected by many, no matter how long it takes.

From all those generations of prophetic seeding, the prophets of our own time have taken up the challenges, however long unfinished.

Harriet Tubman, a slave herself, gave her life to leading slaves to freedom and so enabling others to see them as human beings again.

Dorothy Day recalled the poor to the center of Christian concern and care.

Martin Luther King Jr. healed the hearts of an entire nation by shining light on the forgotten ones and making them visible, making them heard, helping them see themselves as human again. Then he left the rest of his dream to us to finish.

Maryknoll nuns Ita Ford and Maura Clark, Ursuline nun Dorothy Kazel, and laywoman Jean Donovan, missionaries to El Salvador during its civil war, defied the government by continuing to teach the liberation of the poor in an era of ruthless suppression. All four were murdered by the Salvadoran death squads. As a result of their self-giving, the silence of American collusion was broken, the control of the government was broken, and US support of the repression of civil unrest was ended, too.

Dietrich Bonhoeffer, in the middle of the Nazi torrent, refused to accept the theology of Aryan superiority, of Jewish extinction, and was executed for his attempts to dislodge Hitler from power. But the line of Protestant theologians who followed him renewed the prophetic tradition for the rest of us in our time at the worst of times.

The women who started the twenty-first century "Me Too" movement in the United States exposed the commonplace sexual harassment of powerless women by powerful men and so have enabled new dignity, genuine equality, real empowerment, and honest opportunities for women everywhere.

The list is endless. One generation of prophets seeds the next. As the Shaker Antoinette Doolittle puts it, "Every cycle has its prophets as guiding stars; and they are the burning candles of God to light the spiritual temple on earth, for the time being. When they have done their work, they will pass away; but the candlesticks will remain, and other light will be placed in them."

Reflection

It is we for whom the empty candlesticks stand waiting. If, that is, the disciples of this era recognize the prophets' call.

> *"My hope is that my life will declare this meeting open."*
> JUNE JORDAN

12.

WISDOM

Plato may have said it earlier than most, but his insight has been repeated over and over through the centuries. Those who are serious about what they do, or what they hope to see develop, never forget its wisdom: "The wise speak because they have something to say; fools speak because they have to say something." Good intentions do not excuse a person from knowing what they're talking about.

Trust those whose heart has been formed in the scriptures and whose sincere commitment is to the coming of the Reign of God. Plato's warning includes us, you and me, in other words.

In fact, if anything diminishes the power of the prophetic statement, it is a prophetic statement that is wrong about an important issue. Not correct. Not thought out. Not presented carefully—and honestly. The prophet does not come to condemn those who think differently about a thing; the prophet comes to warn, to persuade, to enlighten. The prophet does not come to win by any means available. The prophet's call is to unite the world in an honest understanding of the Word of God for humankind.

People with a prophet's heart do not lead holy armies.

They are holy because they lead hearts, not armies at all. Prophetic spirituality does not set out to pit one side of an issue against those who see the issue from a different perspective. Instead, prophetic spirits come to notify the world of what will happen if, as a people, we continue in the direction we're going. They come to dissuade us from the perils of the positions we are creating for ourselves.

Charles Borromeo, one of the great reformers of the sixteenth century, was clear: "We must meditate before, during, and after everything we do. The prophet says, 'I will pray, and then I will understand.'" The relationship between prophecy and scholarship was clear. The seminaries, colleges, universities, and educational programs Borromeo founded changed the entire tenor of the church from simply clerical to the need, as well, to be thoughtful, knowledgeable, wise.

The prophets of all times and eras must be more than involved bystanders with a brave message—right as it may be. The prophet sets out to enable today's church to understand the spiritual and social implications of the situation, too, so that the message is not lost, the spiritual obligation is clear, and the work is not in vain.

Biblical prophets are also a model for us here. They taught the people as well as goaded them.

In a period when the priests had become privileged and the Temple political, Hosea lamented, "The people perish for want of knowledge." They were not being taught; they were being seduced by the practice of religion but overlooked entirely the righteousness of religion. Like us in our own time, it was far easier for the Jewish people to think that the temple taxes they paid and the altar sacrifices they made, the feast days they kept and the prayers they said, were the essence of religion. The emphasis on teaching justice and the Will of God for the world had all but disappeared.

In our time, too, how much effort has been put into really teaching the legislation on taxes and social safety nets, on fair wages and welfare-to-work programs now being touted as jobs for the poor?

Micah, the biblical prophet in a territory designated as the front line in any attack on Jerusalem, saw people being herded into work camps to do the public works projects of the rich. It was an enslaving and inhumane sight. Micah cried out:

> They are skinning people alive;
> pulling flesh off their bones,
> eating my people's flesh,
> stripping off their skin,
> breaking up their bones,
> chopping them up small
> like flesh for the pot,
> like meat in the stew pan.
>
> (Micah 3:3)

It is a stirring and heartrending description of what happens to people every day, everywhere in this great interconnected, elitist world of ours. Money goes to the top; joblessness in a technological world goes to the bottom. And yet the statistical charts show us "progress" daily. For some, not for all. The numbers are exhilarating— for many—but they put no faces on the bottom of the charts. Neither in Micah's time nor in ours. All we see is that some are profiting and most are not. Indeed, the charts are clear: for some strange reason, the economy favors some but not those who need it most. As taxes come down for the wealthy, the social safety nets come out for few.

How could that possibly happen? Micah's answer is meant for all of us to ponder: he blamed the elders and the religious figures of the day for failing in their duties to teach. He pointed out that religious leadership was concentrating on religious niceties but doing nothing to lead leaders to factor the whole people into their equations. Oblivious of the sins against society that were going on around them, the whole notion of their covenant with God and the creation of Jewish community deteriorated before their eyes. Some were well fed, some were not; some in the society were blessed, some were not; some of the people were free, some were not. We know the picture. We are in the middle of it. In our world, profit increases at a great rate and goes to those who are already secure, though wages at the bottom, where insecurity is a constant companion, seldom change. The working poor get a "minimum wage," never a living wage.

These prophets from thousands of years ago are stern warning for the elders and the prophets of our own time. They leave us with a certain awareness that there is more we must do than decry what we do not like. We must also teach the truths of life, the why of the unjust situation, the downside of the present situation, the will of God for the world that is being violated in the present situation. Most of all, we must also describe the world that must be put in its place.

Prophetic leaders are not required to be economists or politicians—though it would be nice to have a cadre of them. But those are other agendas. The agenda of the prophetic leader is peace and justice, justice and peace. The prophet asks in our time why women are the poorest of the poor—and shows it in neon for all the world to see. The prophet asks why entire peoples, whole segments of the world, are left behind in their efforts to live, to feed their children, to support their families, to get an education, to find decent work, to live free and decent, dignified and happy lives. They force us to see our own role in oppression—internationally, nationally, locally—or at least in the need to speak out for it.

They call us all to a universal bar of judgment and make us choose. Ourselves alone or the poor with us. Our personal welfare or the lives of the have-nots around us, as well. Our race or the world at large.

The role of the prophetic community is to enable a group to study the issues, to become proficient in them, to take a specific, a particular stand, for justice.

Prophetic communities do a great deal more than pray. They study; they teach; they organize others; they add something of the things of God to the situation. They don't just complain about the poor; they do something to feed them. They don't just lament the condition of working mothers; they do something to help them take care of their children. They don't just wish for higher wages for the poor; they advocate for the underpaid. They lobby their legislators and leaders, their pastors and public agencies. They commit to doing something to change their world as well as to talk about it.

Reflection

Prophets ask questions most people do not ask or take the time to pursue. Unfortunately, this is the most important question of all. After we've said our prayers, checked the news, shaken our heads over it, and turned off the TV commentators in despair and disgust, we suddenly remember someone who needs the help we have just read about. Then we ask ourselves what we really stand for—and what we've done to prove it. At that moment, we either become prophets—or simply churchgoers. And that is the ultimate question, the question we must all answer, And you—what are you doing about it?

"Efforts and courage are not enough without purpose and direction."

JOHN F. KENNEDY

13

PROCLAMATION

The answer to the question of who is called to proclaim truth in a silent generation is an easy one: we all are. There is no part of following Jesus the Prophet—of living the Gospels—from which any of us are exempt. Discipleship demands that we each take every Gospel seriously, that we use it to interrogate our own response and reaction to every issue, to every spiritual challenge there. Then and only then can we school ourselves in the mind of Christ. Steeped in the Word, Jesus sets out on the prophet's journey to renew the faith, to protect the defenseless, to develop a vibrantly new theology of God. Therefore, so must we.

The Spirit alive in the Church—the Spirit calling each of us, little by little, to devote ourselves to the coming of the Reign of God—leads us on from grace to grace, showing us life in all its struggles, prodding us to see the world through the eyes of God, requiring us to walk in the footsteps of Jesus the Prophet. The path we so blithely agree to pursue has its demands. It goes through the way of healing the wounded, freeing the oppressed, proclaiming the Word, defining the vision, and confronting the civic hypocrites who put care in the language but seldom in the budget. It is the path of the Jesus who says, "God has sent me to proclaim release to the captives, recovery of sight to the blind, to set at liberty those who are oppressed." And then, quite clearly, "Follow me."

Unfortunately, the vision of Jesus the Prophet has become quite domesticated over the centuries. As life got more comfortable from generation to generation, prophecy became reduced to Christian rituals, to public "witness" of our own private spiritual lives. We learned that the good life was about saying our prayers regularly. We remembered to go to church, for our own salvation was at stake. We kept the great feast days that glued the Christian community together in one worshipping whole and counted on the rumor that membership itself is salvific enough. We knew that our task was to give witness to the role of the spiritual in life by performing special liturgical roles and doing special things to maintain the schools and hospitals and service centers of the institution. All of which were good. Stable. Safe. Very safe. No more skeptical crowds to face, no more public exclusion to worry about now.

No, as time went by, the spiritual path came to be more and more about us: our salvation, our public identity, our eternal rewards, our very special, very safe institutional ministries. Gone were the grubby and the outcast around us, gone were the forgotten or forsaken. These kind, we figured, should do it for themselves. After all, we had. And so we had also become a privileged people in a privileged world, sacrificial, yes; risk-oriented, no. This was not the path of the Jesus who "consorted with sinners and prostitutes." This was the Jesus in the rich man's house begging him: "When you hold a banquet invite the poor, the crippled, the lame, and the blind." Stoop down out of your elite life and bring all the others up with you.

Then, of course, the way becomes plain, becomes shocking. The question becomes searing, Exactly what is the spiritual life for, if not that?

Yet the truth is that every period in the history of spirituality has been in response to a great, growing gap between life as it is and life as God wants it to be for us. In each new age, disciples emerged to meet "the signs of the times."

Monasticism was a response to the breakdown of society after the fall of Rome. Then, with the collapse of civil leadership, monasteries became the center of civic order.

Mendicants, those who lived and worked among the wandering poor, made the creeping disease of poverty impossible to ignore.

Great prophetic figures from the seventeenth to the twentieth century confronted the multiple needs of the fast-growing urban world. They formed groups together that were committed to care for whole segments of society who were now displaced, jobless, and reduced to the squalor of the newly developing cities.

Together they began to treat the wounds of society. They began schools for the poor, for girls, for immigrants. They opened hospitals in the hinterlands and nursed on the battlefields. They built orphanages and old folks homes. All of them great movements of charity and justice.

Indeed, from the time of Amos, the biblical prophet, to the days of our own lives, the concentration of prophetic visionaries has always been dangerously specific. From the opening of the first hospices for the sick in the early Middle Ages to works on behalf of the education of entire societies of the indigent, every age has demonstrated the need for change, for inclusion, for equality, for dignity, for development by the prophets of that age.

In every period, the prophetic task was the same: to interpret the present in light of the Word of God so that new worlds could be envisioned and new attitudes developed that would eventually make the world a better place.

But the needs of God's people today are no less pressing, no more acceptable than they ever were before. Destitute immigrants languish on our borders begging for help. They risk their lives, their families, and even their children to live a decent and dignified life. In the United States, not one state in the union offers a two-bedroom apartment cheaply enough for families who earn a minimum wage to rent it. Which is why, of course, so many young families live in their cars these days waiting to hear a prophet's cry on their behalf.

It is now our task, as individuals, as intentional groups, wherever we are on the social spectrum, to shine a light on their lives and to insist that others see it, too. It is the task of each of us to be their voice until they can be heard themselves. It is the individual prophet's task, whatever we do and wherever we are, to point out their absence in society, their needs, the inequities they bear. It is our task to give them hope, to give them possibility, to help the outcasts to fit in.

The prophetic institutions of the past did their job

well. They became part of a service system that raised one generation of immigrants after another to become part of a pluralistic world.

Then the education and health care that sustained and developed entire populations became mainstream. But there is a price to be paid for being mainstream. "Mainstream" is the word used to define those who are neither too conservative nor too liberal, too far right or too much left to be able to be heard. They are "safe." They are in line with what the system believes is enough for these needy. But the truth is that prophets are never mainstream. "I would prefer that you be hot or cold," Jesus says, "rather than tepid." Prophets see what still isn't happening and din the world until it does.

Prophets are not in between. They hold a completely different vision of life than do most. In fact, they hold the rest of the vision of holiness, the part that seldom is taught in the same breath as charity or morality or good citizenship. They are the other half of Christianity, the forgotten half of the spirituality of the Christian world. They see what's missing in the world around them and set out to see that the world supplies it for those who need it most. They value other ends in life than the ones toward which most of the world strains—for too much wealth, too much power, and too much distance from the daili- ness of the daily.

Reflection

The prophet in this day—facing a world where rugged in- dividualism reigns and those who can't make it on their own are easily forgotten—now must do more than simply serve. They must lead this world beyond its present divisions of race and gender, of national identity and economic class. Yes, the prophet is always out of step with the average response to pain or want or loss or oppression. They are always disturbingly different, always stirring up the consciousness of those left behind, always confronting a world that obstructs them, always on a path toward the Kingdom rather than the palace.

The call today is for all of us to realize that the prophetic tradition has been handed on to each of us to reclaim. The world needs all of us, each of us now, to take our place with Jesus on the road from Galilee to Jerusalem, so that no one's needs and no one's pain is overlooked on the way.

"When you're 17 in the suburbs and know only three gay people, holding hands with your girlfriend is a proclamation."

MARY LAMBERT

14.

VISION

From the time of the biblical prophets, the role of unlikely messengers to contemporary society has been established. "The Spirit of the Lord is upon me," says the biblical prophet Isaiah, "because he has anointed me to bring good tidings to the afflicted." Then he defines the nature of his call to prophecy. "God said to me," he writes, "I have made you a watchman for the house of Israel; whenever you hear a word from my mouth, you shall give them warning from me." The modern church, too, in *Lumen Gentium,* the Vatican II document, *Light to the Nations,* calls the church in our own time to realize that the prophetic life of Jesus "continues not only through the hierarchy but also through the laity whom he made his witnesses to be wrestling against the continual rulers of this darkness, against the spiritual forces of wickedness."

The call of the church to the renewal of the prophetic dimension of the Christian life is clear. But the history of prophets with their churches—ancient and present—is a clouded one. In some instances—in Ireland and Poland, for example—it was churches that sustained the prophets of those societies. When governments sought to stamp out opposition, attempted to destroy the churches themselves, in fact, the fiercest of nonviolent opposition came from the pulpits.

As the Irish are fond of repeating, it was the language, the Gaelic Athletic Association, and the Catholic Church that maintained the identity of the nation through four hundred years of British occupation. The Irish faced the threat of total oblivion in the face of the larger society with which they found themselves in struggle. When their schools were closed, prophetic Irish voices led people to hide their children in the bogs and teach them to read there. When Mass was forbidden, their priests came to celebrate the Eucharist on the "Mass rocks." By using huge boulders lodged in the middle of the hillsides as altars, the congregation could see the enemy coming before an enemy could get to them. Some of those "Mass rocks" can still be found to this day—a reminder of past witness and the kind of courage it took to do it.

In Poland, the churches faced off with their communist overlords and also, in the end, prevailed because the Word of God pronounced in the church meant more to them than the songs of allegiance required by the government.

But in other times and other instances of national oppression, churches became as quiet as mystical moles, showing only the ritualistic side of themselves. The institutional church, for example, seeking new alliance with secular governments, ignored the prophets, like Dietrich Bonhoeffer in Germany and Franz Jägerstätter in Austria, who resisted Hitler. In the United States only the black churches protested slavery, while white churches repeated Paul's: "Slaves, love your masters." In the United States, young prophets who resisted the Vietnam War with all their might were largely ignored by the church, despite the statement of Vatican II in support of it. Their plea for conscientious objection was given no official church support before the government, even while priests and nuns across the country were jailed for their protests.

The question is, How is it that the record is confused on so essential a role as prophetic witness in the modern world? And the answer is not theological. The theology of prophecy, the scriptural basis of prophecy as a function of Christian discipleship, is never in doubt. It is the psychological and social effect of prophecy that intimidate us all.

I remember quite clearly the time during the nuclear arms race and the Vietnam War when my own community, who had adopted a corporate commitment to nuclear disarmament, awoke one morning for prayer just in time to hear ourselves called "feminazis" on the local radio station. Between that and the decline of the student population in our school, the downturn in numbers of benefactors to the community, and the rage of public debate about such positions in the local newspaper in a country that prides itself on "freedom of speech," the question emerged in neon: What is it about unarmed, nonviolent reaction to public policies that can possibly be so threatening?

In some ways, it is actually the very nonviolent character of the dissent that is what makes prophetic dissent so threatening. If a group is violent, it is, some argue, at one level at least, legitimate to attack them. They are obviously a danger to the peace. To abuse groups that are nonviolent, however, as these were, is to make the abusers themselves a menace to the public. Certainly other ways, for other reasons, must be found to silence such antagonists. But why?

It is a volatile situation. Dissent—prophetic spirituality—jeopardizes the status quo. It augurs to endanger a very delicate balance between the authorities of such a society and society itself. What if other people hear such things? What if they listen? What if they set out to change things? Worse, what if they go about it nonviolently? How can such benign danger ever be controlled?

The question is basic to every social structure, and yet other questions, even more dangerous, underlie it: Who is being advantaged by maintaining the present situation and who stands to lose if it changes?

Never doubt that there will be losers aplenty—as there would have been in Israel. If Jesus were allowed to go on voicing the concerns of the peasants, who knows? The peasants may well have risen up against the Temple as well as the empire—which is exactly what they both feared. If Jesus had gone on teaching, rival ideas could have run amok. If Jesus had been allowed to go on arguing with the keepers of the faith about the justice of the religious laws, it could have weakened the prestige of the elders themselves. If people continued to follow Jesus in growing numbers, such new ideas, such dangerous insights could have toppled the tightly held authority of both Temple and Throne.

New ideas anywhere, everywhere, endanger old systems, old rulers. The specter of loss hangs over every crowned head and chairman's chair in sight. They fear the changes, not because the changes are bad but because they are so good. These are the changes that expose the privileges of the Old Guard. They cast doubt on their very moral integrity because if this new thing is right, then the old thing was wrong, or at least deeply lacking. It is the shattering of old shibboleths. It has the smell of failure to it. It fractures the aura of moral impeccability that has for so long favored, applauded, the present system and everything it touches.

Two things need to happen: First, the political maneuvering that makes it possible, for instance, for a congress to hold a country hostage to old or damaging social formulas must be stopped. Second, the commitment to go on "wrestling with the rulers of darkness" must live on in prophetic spirituality today in order to rise ever more loudly and clearly at the first possible moment.

We who descend from the great prophets of Israel and follow in the footsteps of the prophet Jesus know our responsibility to enliven the prophetic tradition in our own communities and social system. One thing is clear: our role is to see that our discipleship does not sink into the status quo.

Indeed, prophecy is a powerful presence, a force that must be handled carefully. This force is essential to the continuing development of both church and nation, people and planet. It brings a power; it exacts a cost.

There is a story: Once upon a time an old woman ran through the streets shouting, "Power, greed, and corruption. Power, greed, and corruption." For a while, people stopped to hear, to think, to discuss the problem. As time went by and nothing happened, they finally went back about their business. Finally, one day, a child stepped in front of the prophet to say as she ran by, "Old woman, no one is listening to you." So, the woman stopped to say, "Oh, I know that." The boy was puzzled. "Then if you know you have failed, why do you go on shouting?" And the old woman answered, "Oh, child, you do not understand. I do not shout in order to change them. I shout so that they cannot change me."

Reflection

The prophetic word is a word that must be tended forever. As Walter Brueggemann teaches, "The prophet does not ask if the vision can be implemented, for questions of implementation are of no consequence until the vision can be imagined." For those who realize the need for change in society if justice, peace, and the Will of God for the world are ever to be achieved, the new vision that must be molded requires immersion in the mind of Jesus and time, time, time.

> *"The only thing worse than being blind is having sight but no vision."*
> HELEN KELLER

15.

FAITH

John Dryden, seventeenth-century English poet, once wrote, "Good people starve for want of impudence." It is a prophet's mantra. Prophecy, Dryden implies, is not simply a matter of mindless risk. It is, at base, a matter of nourishing bold faith in the human ability to make God's message come true. It is also then, further and finally, a matter of excursion into the desert of courageous leadership.

The fascinating—and demanding—dimension of biblical prophecy is that it is God's way, it seems, always to send the weakest among us to do what must be done: Moses, to save the Israelites from slavery; Esther to save the Jewish people from King Ahasuerus; little David to fell the giant Goliath; and we ourselves now, to complete the work only begun by the Creator but forever threatened with failure without us.

In that plan for human development of the divine enterprise lies the place of faith in prophecy. Those who would otherwise do little or nothing about social imbalance find themselves, in the face of the gap between the human and the humane, between the Divine Will for humankind and the human failures to achieve it, impelled to take a stand.

There is no choice now. Something has to be done and someone must do it. Somebody must do something—and that leaves us, leaves me. But how does it happen that the likes of us, tongue-tied and reluctant, suddenly move from silence to public speech? Simple: faith leads us from the dregs of despair to trust again in possibility. It takes the fear that comes from insight and turns it into the conviction that the world must change, that I must change, that I must have something to do with changing it. Faith in God takes us from the fear of public recrimination that grips us to the courage it takes to do God's will for the public good.

Indeed, faith is the single gift that makes prophecy real. Without faith, no prophet could ever have ventured beyond the pain of the present. Without faith there is simply nowhere to go in the midst of breakdown than back to an unacceptable past.

The problem is that the gift of tomorrow does not come complete. Tomorrow is the gift we are given to create for ourselves. In that awareness, in the depths of that kind of faith, lies the energy—the reason—for prophecy. Because we know the will of God for us, the prophet must demand it. If something is to be done, we will have to be the people who do it. Consciousness commits. Once I see what is missing, the kernel of God's will for us, then I must mount the steps of the city to announce its absence and awaken it again.

Like town criers everywhere, it is up to the prophet to sound the alarm.

Faith drives us on, trusting in a future we cannot see but are bound to pursue if our own humanity is ever to come to the fullness Creation designed it to be. No doubt about it: the prophetic vision demands more than insight alone. It demands a steel-willed determination to do something, however little, to bring that awareness to life. If the world in which we live is to be a better one, our spirituality must be about more than seeing what needs to be done. It's about doing something about what is lacking. It's about standing up and speaking out, the lone voice in the room, if necessary, the voice that the others ignore—or worse, laugh at.

Now, on the strength of our faith and the vision it drives in us, we call the faithful to see what we see, to step to its drum, to begin to raise up a new way of being alive. We begin to lead as well as to analyze. We begin to take responsibility for making the Word of God live again, here and now.

We know now that there is no way to merely leave the message about justice or equity or discriminatory policies on a small piece of paper we slide under the president's door. No, prophecy is made of sterner stuff than that. It is about examining the present in the light of the future. It's about seeing what is obstructing the fullness of its coming. To speak a prophetic word is to stare down the opposition, squarely and honestly, in order to present for consideration another way to be a more human human being.

The problem now is determining how to lead a group that does not want to be led. And the answer is to sound the message as clearly, as nonjudgmentally, as we can—and then refuse to go away.

Martin Luther King Jr. was faithful to the vision through beatings, jailings, and death.

Wangari Maathai hugged the trees for thirty-four years hounded by hecklers and subjected to ridicule from one end of the globe to the other. The prophetic act of hugging trees became the inarguable argument as one life-giving forest after another was being denuded for the sake of present profits that would damage future growth.

Nelson Mandela stayed at the post of witness for twenty-seven years and every year became a more silent but ever louder voice.

Dorothy Day carried the warning about war, the calls for peace, and the corresponding plight of the poor in the largest city in the world. From her ghetto in the midst of urban turmoil her beacon became brighter by the year.

Helen Prejean has been walking men on death row to electric chairs and gas chambers for years. But she has also been spending all the time between those moments breaking a path for others to follow after her.

The prophet simply refuses to quit. The prophet does not ever go away. Ever. The voice of the prophet—silent or sure—has the eternal life given by an eternal God.

The prophet is no leader of corporations or armed forces; the prophet leads the most human of human souls. It is a leadership that rings of truth and tradition. Its armies are small bands of prophets everywhere. Its leadership style is not military: it gives no non-negotiable orders. Its leadership role is not quixotic: it is a steadfast, serious call to the righteous, not the reckless.

Prophetic leadership lies in the vision of goodness it

puts before us. It challenges us to compare the lives we live and the dreams we have for them with the commitment to the "liberty and justice for all" we talk about. It sings of peace and equality. It walks where the people walk, carrying their babies and their burdens, their fears and their faith, right into the mouth of the yawning dragon called profit and exploitation, slavery and sexism, power for the few and powerlessness for the many. It awakens people to hope again, to believe again, to begin to re-create the world again.

The leadership of the prophet is fearless because it is rooted in the faith that God's will, will be done. Eventually, certainly, surely, and lovingly.

It took forty years for Moses to find his way through the first desert of oppression, but that vision of liberation lasts until this day. Our deserts are now no wider, no longer, no less difficult to traverse. Neither is it magic nor money that will get us there. No, the prophet's only weapon is vision and voice, time and timelessness. The prophet comes to stay until the last of the hungry are fed and the poor are housed in decent homes and the babies have a future to live for. Then the Reign of God appears on the horizon, just waiting to become real in us. Most important of all, it is we who have called for it. What greater, more noble work can the human being do? What more clearly Christian can a Christian be?

Reflection

"You cannot," Thomas Merton says, "have social order without saints, mystics, and prophets." The call to each of them is yours to have for free—just waiting to be claimed. Only lack of faith can stop us now.

How can people like us, small, powerless, unseen, engage in so great a task? Easy. Our task is to change the opinions of people whose lives have become quietly given over to profit and power rather than to the people who have made their status and wealth possible.

"Isn't it wonderful that two of the most sacred and symbolic plants, the olive and the vine, live on almost nothing—a terrace of limestone, sun and rain."
JANET ERSKINE STUART

16

CONFIDENCE

Moses was a reluctant prophet. Deeply aware in his heart of the need to confront the brutality of the pharaoh in Egypt, he hears the call of God to him: "I have heard the cry of my people and I am sending you to Pharaoh to bring my people out." But scripture says, Moses "was afraid" to look at God.

"Who am I," Moses insists, "that I should go to Pharaoh?" And God says, "I will be with you and this will be your sign." Yet, Moses objects, "Suppose they do not listen to me?" So God shows him how he will be saved if the pharaoh remains obdurate. But Moses is no fool: "If you please, my Lord, I have never been eloquent. I am slow of speech and tongue. If you please, my Lord, send someone else!"

Then, scripture says God became angry with Moses but made his brother Aaron, the one with public speaking skills, his assistant. Consciousness of God's disappointment at Moses's reluctance is a warning meant to be taken seriously.

The Moses story is a charming study. It makes clear how much time it can take to face the fact that something must be done and that we are expected to do it. Did Moses doubt that God was with him? No. Did he doubt that this liberation of the people was God's will? No. Moses believes both the voice and the vision. He doesn't question either. But he shows us something very important for our own lives: Lack of faith in God is one thing, we discover as we grow, but lack of self-confidence can be just as bad. If truth were known, even worse.

Lack of faith in the presence of an invisible God at a difficult time at least makes sense. To lack confidence in the strength I've been given is far more serious than to doubt what I believe will happen though cannot see. To deny the abilities I've been given—thought, insight, wisdom, analysis, understanding, explanation, persuasion— is a virtual sin against creation. It degrades the virtue of humility to a kind of debased self-knowledge. It withholds from the human community the very gifts I have been freely given for its good. Worse, it denies life the effort it takes to make such gifts real. Having gifts is nothing if we don't use them. To praise the Creator for seeding the universe with them is bogus if we ourselves fail to use them to their limits. It is a sin against creation.

Most serious of all, this kind of pious worthlessness itself tends to obstruct the prophetic enterprise. And as Moses found out quickly, God does not like it!

This "O Lord, I am not worthy" argument leads to a distortion of the process of prophetism itself. It claims inability where talent lies dormant and untried. It saves the soul from the grace of failure by never bothering to enter the fray. It denies the fact that whatever talent, insight, vision, strength, and truth that God has given us, God will uphold in us.

The consequences of such an attitude affect far more than the people who decide to absent themselves from the needs of the human race on the grounds of inability. It can bring six other demons with it—perfectionism, false humility, sensitivity, fear, anxiety, and anger—into a group whose hearts are fully engaged, however simple their resources. Dealing with these by-products of human fear may even impinge on the project itself.

Perfectionism, the need to do everything to the highest degree of professionalism in a very slick Madison Avenue world, vitiates our every attempt to make a bad situation better. It brings a sense of failure down on the heads of those whose sincerity is itself the greatest argument of all for success. Instead, more efforts are vetoed where perfectionism stands at the ready to criticize, halt, redo, and amend than can possibly begin, let alone succeed.

A sense of worthlessness pervades the entire movement. Why do it? Who cares? What's the use? Anthems of anguish infect the entire attempt before it can possibly reach its crescendo. It spews self-doubt; it discourages any attempt at real communication with the pharaohs of the world. It undermines the energy it takes to make a difference at anything.

Sensitivity to criticism invades the group. Better to be quiet and simply let things go than try to enlarge a project or improve on a statement or present a public argument for change. The lack of all gifts at full bore slows down the entire undertaking. There is always a sense that something is missing, something is lacking—and with that kind of doubt, the enthusiasm for the message wanes. People begin to drift away. It becomes a team without a team.

Fear and anxiety become more the underlying atmosphere in the venture than full-throated commitment to every small step along the way. Lack of realistic confidence in the goal, in the purpose, in the value of the venture, in our simple efforts to be part of the public conversation, stalk every step. Rather than the singing of the martyrs as they marched into the Coliseum, this great adventure in the process of the new creation becomes a trial, a burden, a bane, a sure failure.

Then anger takes over. Anger at one another over ideas unaccepted, actions undone, time wasted, lack of community support. And underneath it all, anger at the self for becoming involved in a project now apparently adrift and astray. The awareness of the liberation that comes from being part of an idea greater than the self has dimmed. Anger and strain and resentment and fear, fear, fear. Fear of who won't like us for doing this. Fear at being labeled as part of it. Fear of losing, as if losing is not itself simply another contribution to making the world aware of the forces arrayed against the poor, the outcast, the other.

It's time to understand, with Moses, that the God who calls us to our responsibility for the world will also be with us as we shoulder our part in it. That same God will send the help we need, yes, but more than that, faith in that God will make the rough ways smooth. For where there is faith, hope can run wild.

Even our failures, we will come to understand, will be

turned to success in the end. Was it a failure, all those years of Native American, black, and women's voices—whoever the outcasts—that drummed into our consciousness that oppression is a pattern, not an isolated mistake? Was it a failure that each of these situations, protested by so many without success, did in the end accrue to wake us all up to injustice? Did their deaths, their suffering mean nothing if over the years, the body of them cried out to us, "No more" and we were finally able to respond?

Most of all, people-pleasing goes when the worthiness argument disappears. We know who we are and why we do what we do, and no amount of self-doubt or breast beating can stop our journey to justice. Whoever doesn't like it. Whoever tries to stop us from speaking out, from speaking up, over and over again.

Then, like Moses, our time comes and we are ready to be a joyful part of humanity's slow rise to the fullness of itself.

Reflection

There is a moment in the life of the reluctant prophet that we begin to understand, too, what da Vinci meant when he warned us, "Nothing strengthens authority so much as silence." Then our simpering silence ends and the prophetic spirit in us rises. As it is always meant to do. At that moment, we become free. We become unbound by any chains meant to control us: public approval, doubt, the feelings of futility. Then, finally, we really come to know that God is with us, that God is enough for us.

"We can't be afraid of change . . . Holding on to something that is good for you now may be the very reason why you don't have something better."

C. JOY BELL

17

TRADITION

"Impatience," Voltaire wrote, "is the mark of independence, not bondage." Impatience stirs the soul to action. It looks at life with an agitated glance and wants to make it better. It is the first step toward independence of soul. It's the impatience that betrays us. We begin to show the underside of our hearts: what we really think, what we really want, what we really intend to do.

Then the trouble starts. Then the status quo is not enough for us. The gun control issue, the sexual harassment culture, the work-for-welfare kind of indentured servanthood, the academic disparities in a country that requires compulsory education, all manner of inequities—begin to rankle our soul and broaden our vision of the world. Until, finally, we see a better world and commit ourselves to pursuing it. We feel a stronger call than the urge to do more of the same. We get a glimpse behind the veil of social correctness. It happens to any adolescent because it is part of the process of growing up. But it is just as likely to happen in the process of spiritual maturity as well. It is called growth and insight and wisdom. At some point along the line, however settled the tradition we've been raised in, the Tradition itself begins to live in us in new and different ways. Once we have seen the depth and breadth and history of it, we know which parts of it have gone missing.

Over time every tradition desiccates, dries up, gets institutionalized. What was once vibrant and new becomes routine. The best of its contributions to society gets taken for granted. Then, vibrant as it may once have been, we begin to realize that what was once prophetic is now just more of the same.

Much that is new and necessary in society is being ignored, but in the name of a charism long accomplished, we go on doing more of the same. Over the centuries, groups that organized to teach illiterate foreigners, the poor of a society whose illiteracy doomed them to poverty, changed or died out but they did not fail. On the contrary. Those foreigners became integrated into society and are foreigners no longer. The success of those projects became commonplace but, ironically, that very success threatens them now with irrelevance. Only the prophet who comes along crying out loud that they be put to new use can possibly save the mission by changing the ministry. For all the while, the new foreigners—displaced adults, abandoned children, refugees of suspect origin in search of food and houses and jobs—waste away in tents, in refugee camps.

But that is exactly when the prophetic tradition bursts out anew and greening in us. That's when the prophetic comes in. We stop looking at the world through the filters of the last century and begin to look at the world through the very first century of the Tradition. We begin to see the Tradition through the Gospel that roots it and the world that needs it badly, but in new and meaningful ways.

We begin to understand the vision that drove prophets before us to relinquish the standard future, to risk the journey of faith so that others could also live. We can see now what drove their impatience to give the world gifts the world never dreamed would ever come.

At that point, the question finally emerges loud and clear: What are we not doing now that the Tradition, the charism, the first call of Jesus to follow him really demands that we do? But, believe it, that is precisely the moment when the resistance sets in.

The prophet loves the Tradition. But the prophet now sees the demands of the Tradition in new and exacting ways. And, as it did for the biblical prophets, the coming of the vision costs. Ironically, almost invariably, the institution the prophet loves enough to want it to go on living up to its own message, but differently now—rejects the call to new questions, the potential for greater vision. Cuts it off. Silences it. Casts it out.

How many churches, countries, governments, organizations divide in the face of a call to change? Bishops refuse to bless the new works. Priests keep innovative speakers out of their parishes. The church commissions and councils and committees ignore the issues of declining parishes, new needs, even the discussion of new ideas. Completely.

Nothing could be more painful, more likely to break the prophet's heart, more likely to distort the prophecy itself than to be separated from the very clay that shaped her. The prophet who fails to persevere despite the institution's disapproval surrenders the prophetic moment.

How and why could that happen? The answer itself is painful: It happens because the choice is now between the need for human security and the consciousness of the divine imperative in life. The need to be who I know myself to be is of the essence of human development. By choosing the kind of approval and inclusion that requires the damping of the message, the vocation of the messenger dies incognito. And with it goes the full spiritual development of the prophet him/herself. Rejection is the ultimate punishment: it cuts the prophet's birthright off at the root. Identity becomes a basic issue. Who am I if what called me, named me, marked me, is no longer the aim and the measure of my existence? Who am I then?

The loss of community, of somewhere to go, somewhere to call home, leaves the prophet adrift. It undermines certainty. It drains the heart of purpose. To find the place where someone knows who I am and what I am talking about and why I am saying what I say becomes paramount. To have to look for community outside what I have always known to be community is also a damning condition itself.

The lack of understanding pierces the heart. There are those who call it pride. Some name it arrogance. Few realize that it is a call created by the Tradition and so is being driven by the Tradition itself. The prophet becomes a country of one. The Amish call it shunning. Churches call it excommunication. Temples call it secularization. And everywhere the foundation weakens. Great, highly respected, long-successful prophetic groups implode under the weight of trying to decide whether to continue past goals or pursue the clearly neglected new ones. There is no denying the pain or the hurt and anger and sadness that attends it. There are no cures for such rejection.

But there is a built-in balm. It is in the lives of the prophets and psalmists themselves. Scripture is full of the stories of these visionaries whose very vision was the reason for their abandonment. There the feelings of loss and faith, of pain and self-giving, are affirmed. In them we can see God's will brought to fulfillment, even if not in the life of the prophet who told of it.

The prophet must reject the rejections. To stay in the system while the system itself comes to see a new way of fulfilling the promise to be faithful gives a new kind of depth, of glue, to its growth. It says that the charism is free to grow in many directions. The more the better. Then seers from every perspective can become engaged together in the great work of redeeming the time.

It's important to find living models of rejection in order to live through it well. "If you want to smell sweet," the Sufi says, "stay close to the seller of perfumes." The models, the icons of the charism, both past and present, provide the footprints it takes to go a path alone. Thomas Merton was rejected even by many of his brothers in community. Dorothy Day was scorned by the bishops but persisted in shining a light into the dark corners of poverty. Male theologians like Roy Bourgeois supported women's arguments for Roman Catholic ordination and were denied teaching positions in the church. Sister Theresa Kane called on the papacy to open ministries to women and was censored for it, too. But they all went on to lead in other ways. It is the paradox of prophecy that what calls us to newness also provides a sense of the boundaries that mark the distance between rebellion and prophecy. It's to them we point for affirmation.

Finally, it's important to reach out to those who see the same world vision as we do—for support, of course, but for direction and information as well. It is a long journey to a new place of hope. It takes initiative, creativity, and persistence to go the entire way alone. Through it all, companions make the journey more an adventure than a mistake. To be on the way to a new land in the name of the God of Abraham and Moses, Mary and Joseph, gives new meaning to life. By all means, go.

Simply remember as you go, that you have already seen the Promised Land in your heart. Know that you, too, are led by the charism to find it. Realize, then, that whatever the cost, the pain of the way is worth it.

This great moment of rejection happens for a reason. Sometimes it is about sending you on a path you would not travel but without which you can never complete the enterprise. And even if not that, it is about your own opportunity to evolve beyond your old self. There is nothing but growth and insight and wisdom on this road. Be not afraid.

Reflection

"Where there are no prophets," Alan Richardson, Christian Apologist, maintains, "there can be no special revelation." Remember always that it is the revelation you are about, not yourself, not the preservation of the institution, not the past. It is the revelation seeking to be born again in you, through you newly, for which you go on. Then life will be forever full, however different, and carry with it the memory of the Jesus who cured the daughter of the Roman soldier and walked with groups for which he was condemned. Better that than to be approved for refusing to entertain the voice of the Spirit in the world.

"We must have the courage to let go of the past if we are going to grasp the future."
DAVID DENOTARIS

18

PROPHETS THEN, PROPHETS NOW

Charles Spurgeon wrote, "We are all, at times, unconscious prophets." It's a lovely thought, an intriguing one, but, frankly, a little too loose to be a very demanding concept. The world cannot afford "unconscious prophets" much longer. On the contrary. We need to decide on which areas of change we ourselves want to concentrate. We are here to be messengers of God. We are here to be a rudder on the ship of life. We are meant to be heralds and watch guards, lovers and followers of the Jesus who called all of Israel to remember the poor, save the women, embrace the outliers, consort with the foreigners, and wrestle the Law to the ground of compassion. It is a most exalted—most demanding, most dangerous—calling. But without it, we will never become the whole of ourselves.

Unless and until we accept the prophet's call, we may be great caretakers, good scholars, sincere seekers, fine people, but we will never be fully "spiritual." We will be liked, admired, respected, and—safe. But truly spiritual? Not completely.

The question is, Whose respect would we risk to have? Would we want to be found on the side of the peacemakers, the single women, the discriminated against, the immigrants, the thinkers and the changers of a society whose corporate CEOs get richer every day while the middle class disappears and the poor get more destitute by the hour?

In fact, does anyone know anymore, just by looking at what we're doing, whose side we are on? And how would they prove it?

The truth is that every generation and every segment of society has its prophets. These people, we recount with pride, were the builders and truth-tellers who exposed corruption and worked with the underlings of society. They were missionaries and holy pioneers, spiritual leaders and protectors of the oppressed. Because of them, the entire society was better in the end—no matter how much resistance they faced as they began their small and local projects for peace, justice, and equality. They went into the wilderness to reach boundaries still unmarked and communities yet to be served. They climbed mountains to get to cut-off valleys and the peasants locked within them. They left Europe to follow emigrant populations to lands none of them knew.

They built a new church in a new world, opened services everywhere for the last and the least, and became the voice of the masses. They were the prophets of the time. They went everywhere and did anything that needed to be done. And they did it all for very little remuneration and no guarantees of success, whatever that might look like in an unshaped world.

They were prophetic acts unseen before that time.

But now everything has changed. In a highly institutionalized society, institutions are largely controlled by the state, whatever they are and whoever is running them. So where is society's prophetic dimension now? Who needs it? What message does it bear as it goes? Most of all, in whose behalf does it function?

In the mid-twentieth century, armies of religious dispersed into whole other arenas: public service sectors, soup kitchens, peace groups, housing units for the poor elderly, childcare facilities, adult education programs in inner cities, legal services for the poor, international human rights programs, mobile medical units. It was a truly prophetic call now to listen to the needs of the world, to critique the systems and leadership that controlled them, to be voice for the voiceless.

Then, an even more astounding surge in society emerged. Streams of lay disciples, as had been common to Protestant congregations before them, took up the cause as well. Even more impacting, interfaith groups became crucial to the flow of immigrants and refugees that moved back and forth across the planet in greater numbers than in any other time of recorded history. Ecology groups spoke up to save the planet. Peace groups began to teach tactics of nonviolent resistance in contradistinction to all the guerrilla wars and terrorist activities on the globe.

Now both religious and lay prophets went out alone or in mixed groups to open small advocacy and service centers. And most of all, they went into other institutions as well.

The conclusion was obvious: Buildings and professional ministries are not what prophecy is about. They may flow out of a prophetic call, but the work itself is no substitute for prophecy in a decaying world. Prophecy is about being a clear voice about a specific need. It is about identifying the clouding forces on the human horizon.

Associations of people, either as a collective or as committed individuals who pledge to give special attention to particular issues—to ecology, or women, or homelessness, or enculturation of refugees—to whatever cries for justice and help if life is going to be good for all, not just for some—are prophetic.

Bands of disciples who speak with one voice on issues closest to their hearts—hospitality and housing, the education and promotion of women, the equal treatment of men whatever their color, the care of the poor, the bringing of peace, the rehabilitation of the incarcerated—are the new band of prophets. They are bonded to the issues and to one another—either communally or technologically. They are the new messengers of the Word of God to us all.

All of these massive global issues now need the power of numbers—a corporate commitment—to make the world aware of what is wanting there. They need the clarity of focus that refuses to let the idea drift away from the consciousness of the politicians, the benefactors, the administrators, the directors, the police who are needed to bring special support to the weakest of society. They need your name and mine, your voice and mine, your care and mine, your commitment and mine.

This time the difference is that we are all free to be public prophets—lay and religious together. More than that, we can all be where the issues are, but without the

added weight of caring for expensive facilities and defined populations. Together in new and effective ways,
today's prophets go on shaking and moving and changing the world. Only this time they are doing it differently.
They are traveling light.

Bertrand Russell once wrote: "Order, unity, and con-
tinuity are human inventions." And he was right. There
is no doubt that we can invent them again. The identi-
fication of concerns common to the historical themes
of the Beatitudes, Jesus' own constitution of Christianity, but specific to this age and time, brings order to our
own lives. Most of all, they give volume to our own small
voices, and best of all, they model the assurance of conti-
nuity from one age to another.

A prophetic spiritual life does not demand a corpo-
ration or a campus, big buildings or great facilities to
change the world. Now the call is for a clear and common
voice to challenge oppression and discrimination of any
kind, to call out injustice and invisibility of every kind.
To hold up group after group in the face of the virulent
racism and prejudice that comes with the movement of
whole populations in a dry, waterless, economically enslaved, and warring world. It is that new prophetic voice
for which the world is waiting. It is the voices of Amos
and Hosea, Isaiah and Micah, Jeremiah, Ezekiel, and now
yours that is needed to change the world.

Reflection

What does a prophet do? A prophet cries out, cries out,
cries out. Without fear. Without care for cost. Without

end. Dear Prophet, for the sake of the children, for the sake of the world, for the sake of the gospel, Cry out.

> "Be not a whisper that is lost in the wind; be a voice that is heard above the storms of life."
> —MAIMONIDES

ACKNOWLEDGMENTS

The Time Is Now is the byproduct of years in a monastery, steeped in the scriptures. Praying psalms of suffering and listening to the call, the warnings, the cry of the poor of which the prophets of the Hebrew Testament spoke, the more I realized that the situations were not new ones.

These prophets talked of worlds steeped in violent wars. They argued the problems of the poor: slave labor, unjust wages, grueling work hours, exploitation.

They criticized the high priests and their collusion with the wealthy, their exercise of Temple taxes even for those who could barely afford the sacrifices they were called to make.

They talked about oppression and injustice everywhere. They castigated those who preached religion but ignored its heart.

And all the while as I prayed the prayers, I was watching this era's prophets. They were marching in the streets outside the chapel door to end the terror of war; eating at segregated lunch counters; praying on the steps of churches that forbade altar girls; opening soup kitchens; and carrying the toddlers of farmworker families out of the fields and into Head Start Programs in the hope that these children would have more opportunities to live a more dignified and decent life than their parents had.

I acknowledged the effect of all these courageous, patient people on my own life.

And then I realized the problem: It is so comforting to follow Jesus the Healer, the Jesus who cures the sick and multiplies the fish and even raised women, in all their uselessness, from the dead. But that is only half what it means to do the will of God. Jesus the Healer, you see, is also Jesus the Prophet who contended with those in the Temple and the Throne who condemned his condemnation of the system.

And so my hope for this book is that we might all see the place of prophetic spirituality in our own spiritual lives. "Those who risk nothing risk much more," the proverb teaches. Like integrity. Like authenticity. Like the fullness of life.

It is an important dimension of our spiritual lives, obviously. So I am particularly grateful for all the people who contributed to the presentation of this work. The readers—Mary Lou Kownacki, OSB; Dr. Gail Freyne; Dr. Kathleen Schatzberg; and Susan Doubet, OSB—gave this work another level of contact with the soul of the world as we know it today. They wrestled through every word of the manuscript with the intensity of scholars and saints. I am forever grateful.

My editor, Gary Jansen, brought his usual care and critical eye to the presentation and to the content. He sees it as another look at spirituality and moral responsibility as we need it today. Ashley Hong brought the patience of Job to every topic. It's impossible for a writer not to be grateful for people who bring as much attention to a manuscript as the writer herself.

The Penguin Random House staff, in general—in advertising, communication, artistry, and layout—is both intense and delightful to work with. In the end, all of these people have invested their own life with mine in this process. I can never thank them enough.

My one last hope for this book is that groups will read it together and bring the same kind of spiritual fire to it that this staff and readers did. Then we may all become the shapers of the world we want and as responsible for life as we are meant to be.

ABOUT THE AUTHOR

JOAN CHITTISTER, OSB, is one of the best known and best loved writers, international speakers, and influential leaders of this age. Sister Joan has dedicated her life to being a courageous advocate for justice, peace, and equality, especially for women—in church and in society. She is known internationally as a speaker and organizer, and is considered "one of the most influential religious and social leaders of our time."

She has a master's degree from the University of Notre Dame, a Ph.D. in speech communication from Penn State University, and was an elected fellow at Cambridge University. She was prioress of her community, the Benedictine Sisters of Erie, Pennsylvania for twelve years, was president of the Leadership Conference of Women Religious, and is currently co-chair of the Global Peace Initiative of Women, a partner organization of the UN that works to develop a worldwide network of women peace builders. As co-chair of this group, Sister Joan has facilitated gatherings of spiritual leaders throughout the Middle East, Asia, Africa, the Far East, and Europe in an effort to spread an interfaith commitment to peace building, equality, and justice for all.

Sister Joan has written more than sixty books, including *Radical Spirit* (2017), *Between the Dark and the Daylight* (2015), and *Following the Path* (2012) from Penguin Random House.